Good Lu

Love,

Patty

COMMON-SENSE SELLING

JOE CASALE

Longman Financial Services Publishing
a division of Longman Financial Services Institute, Inc.

While a great deal of care has been taken to provide accurate and current information, the ideas, suggestions, general principles and conclusions presented in this book are subject to local, state and federal laws and regulations, court cases and any revisions of same. The reader is thus urged to consult legal counsel regarding any points of law—this publication should not be used as a substitute for competent legal advice.

Executive Editor: Kathleen A. Welton
Project Editor: Lois Smit
Interior Design: Ophelia M. Chambliss-Jones
Cover Design: Renée Klyczek

© 1989 by Longman Group USA Inc.

Published by Longman Financial Services Publishing
a division of Longman Financial Services Institute, Inc.

Printed in the United States of America.

89 90 91 10 9 8 7 6 5 4 3 2 1

Library of Congress Cataloging-in-Publication Data

Casale, Joe.
    Common-sense selling / Joe Casale.
        p.   cm.
    Includes index.
    ISBN 0-88462-863-9
        1. Insurance—Agents.   I. Title.
HG8091.C37   1989
    368'.0068'8—dc19   89-2363
                                                        CIP

Dedication

When you put this much effort into anything, the dedication is easy.

For my wife Doris (my beloved "Crashie") and my wonderful kids: Francis, Cecilia and Joseph. Thank you all for giving so much meaning to my life.

Contents

Acknowledgments

I owe so many thanks to so many people that I'm terrified that I'll leave someone out. If I have over-looked someone, please be assured you were forgotten only in print and not in my heart.

Thanks to Allen Pathmarajah, general manager (president) of Great Eastern Life Assurance Company in Singapore, who first encouraged me to write this book.

Thanks to my marvelous wife, Doris, whose honest criticism led me to trash my first efforts and start over with a different format.

Thanks to Sarah Moriarty for her help in editing, formatting, checking and otherwise getting a finished product presentable enough to send to a publisher.

Thanks to two long-time inspirational friends, John Savage and Sid Freidman, as well as Dave Hetrick, John Gummere, CEO of Phoenix Mutual, and many others who encouraged me after reading the first proofs.

Thanks to my brother-in-law and close friend, Jack O'Connor, who lent the wisdom of his 30 years in journalism to this effort.

Thanks finally to Longman Financial Services Publishing and especially to Kathy Welton for having the confidence in me to publish this book.

Preface

I don't know about you, but the insurance business is not what I planned for my life's work. If you start with my overwhelming desire to be a cowboy at age six, and proceed through center fielder of the New York Yankees, lawyer, priest, Marine and debonair international secret agent, you will cover most of the things I ever gave a thought to doing for my career. The fact is, I never thought much at all in terms of "career" I was always too busy doing whatever I was doing.

I woke up one day and realized I'd better figure out something quick. I was 31 years old, married, a father and unemployed. I needed to make money. A couple of previous job interviews convinced me that if I wanted to make a lot of money fast, I'd have to sell something. Insurance was a field I knew nothing about, but a friend told me that if I worked hard I could make a lot of money. I chose insurance and couldn't be happier about it. My career in this business has afforded a lifestyle for me and my family that transcends my wildest dreams.

I was born in the East Harlem section of Manhattan. My parents were not poor (at least I didn't think so), but we had no extra money and we ate a lot of macaroni. A new suit of clothes every Easter constituted a spending spree for us. What I had in overabundance was love. When you have that, you don't notice all the things you don't have, which people these days seem to think they're entitled to. My mom and dad both worked, and, when I was old enough, I just hung out in the neighborhood until someone came home. I thought that was pretty neat. Nobody told me I was a latchkey kid. No kid was ever showered with more real love and encouragement from his parents than I was. I couldn't tell you in a thousand pages how much that meant to me.

I went to Holy Cross College in Worcester, Massachusetts. The Jesuits taught me how to think clearly and logically, and I'll be forever indebted to them for that. I have to say that clear thinking is sometimes an aggravating virtue because you develop a very low tolerance for a lot of the garbage that passes your way as "educated thought." The good fathers also insisted on clarity of expression. They forced you to write and speak well. God bless them for that.

After college I went into the Marine Corps. They taught me discipline. The physical and mental demands of the Marine Corps showed me what I was capable of. l learned what it meant to be a man among men and to be up front with people. Those lessons have never been forgotten. The Corps is a secular and not a religious organization, but you learned after a while that the discipline inherent in the Marine code of conduct truly sets you free. I suppose you can learn that lesson elsewhere, but I chose not to be a monk.

In 1965, just a few months before my 30th birthday, I married the former Doris O'Brien. It was the smartest thing I've ever done. That marvelous lady has helped me to be the best I can be. Whatever success I have enjoyed would not have been possible without her. Her wisdom and compassion have aided me beyond my ability to describe it.

That's enough about me. I just wanted the readers of this book to know that I didn't step off a yacht to sell to Dad's friends at the "club." I've known about money and/or the lack of it for a long time. My approach to our business is not based on theory or textbook solutions. Common-sense solutions to real-life problems are what I deal in. No smoke, no fluff, no mystique.

Introduction

You may not have ever thought about it this way, but the bottom line of just about every insurance sale is momma and the kids. If you keep the basics in mind and work hard enough, you'll do well. After all, we deal in basics. Think about this:

- We provide money for family income.
- We provide money for kids' educations.
- We provide money to keep the business in the family.
- We provide money to keep the family independent of a former partner.
- We provide money for retirement.
- We provide money in case of disability or hospitalization.
- We provide money to pay taxes so the family can keep its property.

As you probably guessed from the list above, our job is to provide money. Our product lets us do that better than anyone else. This little book is designed to help you *keep it simple*. Enjoy!

It may be appropriate at this point to point out that, with the exception of a few ladies who happen to be married to my clients, I don't have any female clients. Since this book is about my sales operation and my agency, you will not find many references to females. I refuse to engage in the he/she game, and I don't routinely use the word *salesperson*.

To the best of my knowledge, it is still correct to use masculine pronouns generically. If a surge of paranoia leads you to think I'm a sexist, consider the following.

My mother worked full time from the time she was 13 until she retired last year at 72. She didn't work out of any sense of liberation. She worked to put food on the table—first in her parents' home and then in ours.

My father has always done most of the cooking in our house and his share of the shopping, cleaning, etc. This in addition to working a regular job.

As for me, I don't cook. But I dare say that I've set more tables, washed more dishes and changed more diapers than many of the sensitive souls who might take offense at my not saying "he/she."

I also don't say "surviving spouse" when I mean "wife." You see, I'm not overly concerned about widowers. The few I know are having a great time. I worry about widows. They have a lot tougher row to hoe than their male counterparts. Having said that, if you are still offended I can't help you. Have a drink!

Chapter 1

Basic Truths

A friend of mine is fond of saying that if two people agree on everything, one of them isn't needed. Nonetheless, I think it is necessary to have a basic set of beliefs that form the foundation of your daily activity. While there are plenty of things in this world that are relative, financial common sense isn't one of them. (As an aside, I don't think morals and ethics are relative, either.) With that in mind, consider the following:

ALL INTELLIGENT PLANNING STARTS WITH A GOAL OR OBJECTIVE.

After all, I can't tell you how to get there if you don't know where you are going.

MOST PEOPLE DON'T HAVE ANY MONEY.

You could argue about the literal merit of that statement, but my experience is that it is generally true. Remember, I'm talking about cash or its equivalent—dollars you can spend *right now* if you have to.

CASH IS KING.

All too often, the guy with the fancy toys has to save up to weigh himself. Of course if you were conscious on October 19, 1987, you know that maintaining even a larger investment portfolio without a cash reserve is a very dangerous game. If you weren't conscious then, the stock market dropped 500 points. One guy killed himself, and another guy killed his broker and then killed himself. Another joyous day on Wall Street.

KNOWLEDGE IS POWER.

The more you know about what you are doing, the simpler will be your explanation to your client. Remember the blue-book exams you took in school? The less you knew about the answer to the question, the more you wrote, hoping to put in a few things the teacher liked. When you knew the answer—BAM!—you wrote it down and went on to the next question. That's what your knowledge should let you do—express the essentials and go on.

MOST OBJECTIONS TO LIFE INSURANCE BOIL DOWN TO AN UNWILLINGNESS TO PAY THE PREMIUM.

I've never met anyone who didn't want the insurance; they just didn't want to pay for it.

INSURANCE IS MANY TIMES THE BEST AND SOMETIMES THE ONLY SOLUTION TO A FINANCIAL PROBLEM.

No other product or financial tool can put exactly the amount needed where it is needed at the exact time it is needed. Only life insurance.

WE ARE SELLING TIME!

Most people are convinced that if they have enough productive time, they will make enough money to take care of their families. They are probably right! That is a big *if*, however. No one is guaranteed the time. That is what makes insurance so perfect.

IF YOU DON'T GET THE TIME, WE GIVE YOU THE MONEY.

IF YOU GET THE TIME, WE GIVE YOU YOUR MONEY BACK.

Of course when you talk about giving the money back, you are talking about whole life. If you have been in this business for more than a week you already know why permanent life insurance is one of the great bargains in the financial world. As John Savage sums up best, "Term insurance is like wetting the bed. It is immediate relief but not a good long-term solution."

YOU ARE GOING TO WORK A LONG TIME BEFORE YOU FIND MANY WIDOWS AND ORPHANS WITH TOO MUCH MONEY!

Remember, that's the business we're in. We provide money for momma and the kids. I don't care what kind of fancy name we put on our sale: stock redemption, deferred compensation, pension, estate planning and so on. The bottom line is this: What we are doing is designed ultimately to safeguard the financial security of the client's family. Almost always, it's momma and the kids.

Chapter 2

Young People

Do you remember when you first were on your own? All of a sudden, Mom wasn't going to wash your underwear, cook your meals or make your bed. You didn't care. Right? You were free! You had a job, money in your pocket, plenty of friends of both sexes to share it with you, and alleluia! your own apartment. You had plans to buy a car and take a great vacation. What do you suppose was one of the last things on your priority list? Right again—planning for your own future financial security. Was that bad? Were you a freak? I think it was perfectly normal. It came with the territory. What was going to happen ten, twenty or more years down the line was not one of your problems. Well, it was—you just didn't know it.

If you think it is any different today, think again. There is nothing more constant than the attitudes of young people regarding themselves and their lifestyles.

You may find young people more career conscious today than they were in the fifties and sixties, but they are still interested in getting all those goodies that may have escaped them before they were on their own. You probably had the same list: apartment, sports car, fancy vacations, etc.

I wish someone had sat me down when I was 21 or so and gone over the financial facts of life. I'm sure I would have been a lot better off at age 30 when I found myself married, penniless and with no prospects. Here are some of the things I needed to hear and that young people need to hear today:

- They need to accumulate money (whether married or single).
- They need to begin an intelligent life-insurance program.
- They need to protect their incomes with a maximum affordable disability-income insurance policy.

Of course, no young guy or girl wants to hear all that, so you have to coordinate what they want to do and what they should do. The average young person isn't worried about retirement planning or funding college educations for kids. These things are so many years away that it seems silly to worry about them now.

Their goals are usually short term and important to them right now. That is perfectly normal. You will do a lot better with these young folks if you accept their thinking and work with it.

You should convince young clients to build a safety net so that once they have those things, like a new car or better apartment, they won't have to lose them through temporary setbacks like being laid off from work or being fired or becoming disabled. It could just happen that on one of those great vacations in Aspen they become disabled and find themselves out of work for three or four months or more.

There is a life-insurance program of modest cost which can take your young clients almost all the way through life without changing a thing. Remember, I said "almost." This contract does a lot of things. It accumulates a lot of cash, it builds a very impressive death benefit and it can provide a substantial boost to a person's expected retirement income. Cradle to grave! The contract I'm talking about is life fully paid at 65.

With an L-65 contract, the first-year premium pays for the death benefit. From that point on, the cash value increase equals or exceeds the premium every year. (At some younger ages there is a glitch in year three). Even if future tax legislation should take away some of the tax benefits of contracts like this, one thing is sure: Money saved, taxable or not, is better than no money saved. Without an adequate cash reserve, there can be no safety net.

Look at the illustration of L-65 in table 2–1. This is a very versatile contract and it provides a sizable amount of cash at age 65. As the young person in the

---

TABLE 2–1 Life Paid Up At 65 Illustration: Variable Loan Rate			
Dividends to purchase paid-up additions			Male, Age 25
Base policy face amount: $155,150			Nonsmoker
Annual premium payable: $2,400 to age 65			
Policy Year	Net After-Tax Insurance Outlay	Net Cash Value	Net Death Benefit
1	$ 2,400	$ 0	$ 155,150
2	2,400	2,469	160,737
3	2,400	4,768	164,333
4	2,400	7,126	168,737
5	2,400	9,976	174,444
Sum 5	12,000	9,976	174,444
Sum 10	24,000	31,456	222,899
Sum 15	36,000	67,950	299,051
Sum 20	48,000	124,607	405,838
Sum 25	60,000	211,435	553,395
Sum 30	72,000	343,136	754,913
Sum 35	84,000	542,856	1,031,103
Sum 40	96,000	843,664	1,412,069 (age 65)
41	−51,564	860,291	1,445,862
42	−51,564	877,268	1,480,038
43	−51,564	894,440	1,514,465
44	−51,564	911,667	1,549,140
45	−51,564	928,825	1,584,244
Sum 45	−161,821	928,825	1,584,244
Sum 50	−419,642	1,005,124	1,750,282
Sum 55	−677,463	1,022,091	1,838,204
Sum 60	−935,284	883,098	1,753,599
Sum 65	−1,193,105	422,615	1,266,532 (age 90)

NOTE: Amounts not shown as guaranteed are based on our current interest-sensitive dividend scale and are neither guaranteed nor estimates for the future. This proposal is not a contract and is subject to the contract provisions that are stated in the policy.
SOURCE: Phoenix Mutual Life Insurance Company.

illustration gets older he may be able to increase his deposit to L-65, and the cash will accumulate faster and his safety net will get stronger. There are simply no good reasons not to start this program.

Our first goal for the client in the table is savings, and not insurance, so we start with a $155,150 death benefit. With no increase in premium, his death benefit at age 65 is $1,412,069. That's a lot of money even if you say it fast! Now it starts getting really wild. At age 65 he begins taking out $51,564 a year *tax-free*. He can do that for 25 years, until he is 90, and if he dies on his 90th birthday, the death benefit is still over $1 million. Try that at your local savings and loan!

I find this program preferable to IRAs. I would feel that way even if the IRA rules had not been changed by the new Tax Reform Act of 1986. With this contract, the money is available if needed without any penalty. Young people should not be forced to tie up their money for 30 to 40 years. Tables 2–2 and 2–3 show a nonqualified IRA presentation that I have made successfully, using the L-65 contract.

The cash accumulation is only the first part of the safety net. Part two, as you might have guessed, is a strong disability-income insurance (DI) contract. No young person should be without disability income. While it is true that at this stage of their lives younger people may not have high levels of responsibility, it is also true that this is a time for acquisitions, like the new car and the new apartment we mentioned. No young person wants to have to give up his car or his apartment. That is just what might happen if all of a sudden the cash flow stops. Disability-income insurance is typically not an expensive proposition. For example, a 25-year-old man making $30,000 a year can get up to $1,800 per month disability income with a benefit to age 65 and pay only $576 per year. That's $48 per month.

TABLE 2–2	Has the Tax Reform Act of 1986 Taken Away Your Tax-Deductible IRA? (Then Compare It with the IRA Alternative!)	
	IRA	IRA Alternative
Are contributions tax-deductible?	No[a]	No
Are rates of return competitive?	Yes	Yes
Can annual contributions exceed $2,000 per individual?	No	Yes
Are postretirement benefits tax-free?	No	Yes
Can benefits be taken before age 59½ without substantial penalty?	No	Yes
Can benefits be borrowed?	No	Yes
Is there a preretirement death benefit?	No	Yes
Are contributions self-completing if disabled?	No	Yes[b]

[a]If a participant in a pension plan and: if single and AGI exceeds $35,000 or if married and AGI exceeds $50,000.
[b]At a small additional cost.

A young person in that situation agreeing to put aside ten percent of earned income, $3,000, could spend $2,400 a year on L-65 and $600 on DI and build a very attractive safety net under all of his other objectives, goals, acquisitions and mistakes.

This program, if started at an early enough age, can do the job all by itself for a lot of people.

There is no question that a change in the tax laws could alter the nature of this plan somewhat, but not enough to detract from its basic appeal. Look at the cash accumulated 20 years down the line, when our young client is 45, and maybe has a child ready to enter college. Do you think that $125,000 will come in handy? How about as a down payment on a new home,

TABLE 2–3 Comparison of a Nondeductible IRA with Alternative Investments

	IRA	Muni-Bond Fund	Deferred Annuity	Series EE Bonds	L-65 Contract
Are contributions tax-deductible?	No[a]	No	No	No	No
Are the interest, dividends and so on tax-advantaged?	Yes[b]	Yes[b]	Yes[b]	Yes[b]	Yes[c]
Are rates of return competitive?	Yes	Yes	Yes	Yes	Yes
Can individual contributions exceed $2,000 per individual?	No	Yes	Yes	Yes	Yes
Can benefits be taken on a tax-free basis?	No	Yes	No	No	Yes
Can benefits be taken before age 59½ without penalty?	No	Yes	No	Yes	Yes
Can benefits be borrowed?	No	No	No	No	Yes
Is there a pre-retirement death benefit?	No	No	No	No	Yes
Can contributions be self-completing if disabled?	No	No	No	No	Yes
A perfect score is nine *yes* answers:	2	5	3	4	8

If a participant in a pension plan and: if single and AGI exceeds $35,000 or if married and AGI exceed ;50,000.
Tax-deferred.
Tax-deferred or tax-free.

or a vacation retreat? Is there anyone reading this book who couldn't use an extra $125,000?

So remember that young people, particularly young *single* people, have a need for our services and our products. If you talk to them reasonably and suggest affordable programs that make sense, both you and your young clients will be very happy with the results.

Two things happen to most young people:

They get older (we hope!).

They get married (probably).

When those things happen, their needs grow and they need your help even more. So stay with them. Those ideal, target-market, affluent, business-owner, prospects weren't born at age 50. They started young! If you helped them when they had nothing, they will remember you when they have it all. These young men and women are out there waiting for your call. Don't let them down.

Chapter 3

The Family

When my wife and I got married, we had next to nothing. I was working in a franchise restaurant and making about $140 a week. My wife was a secretary at a local firm for about $75 a week. Just in case you don't know, that wasn't very good money in 1965 either.

It wasn't long before my wife was expecting our first child, and we had to learn to handle a growing expense load with one less income. Well, the only thing different today is that the incomes are higher and people seem to want more things. We kept our own counsel and worked it out together. However, we sure could have used some help! Modern families, young and old, are just the same now as they were then. They need help.

The family is the cornerstone of a civilized society, and regardless of how sophisticated we think our sales may be, what we do always affects a family's well-being. Financial security is what we bring to the table. I am not sure that I have the inclination to recount all of the wacky as well as sobering incidents that have happened to me over the years. But I'll start with one or two that occurred very early in my career and that had a profound influence on my attitudes about life insurance, money and financial common sense.

When World War II was over and my dad came home from the Philippines, his first goal was to take his family out of the city (they call my old neighborhood a ghetto now) and buy a home in the "country."

In 1948 we moved to a small town called Harrison, New York. It was definitely different. There were no daily street fights or gangs; and, although they had no Police Athletic League on the corner, they did have a youth center. The town had a recreation director named Frank Sollazzo. I loved him. He taught me how to play baseball. He encouraged me constantly and often bought me equipment with his own money. I maintained a close relationship with Frank, his wife Peggy and their four sons.

One day Frank came home from work hot and thirsty. He went to his kitchen sink to get a glass of water. He grabbed the sink, fell to the ground and died. He had suffered a massive coronary. There had been no warning, no shortness of breath or chest pains.

One moment a picture of health, the next minute dead. I attended the wake each night and cried as I had never cried before. Outside of my own family, Frank had treated me as well or better than anyone I had ever known. Now he was gone. He was about 54 years old.

His wife, who had spent her whole life devoted to the care of her husband and children, had to find a job. She had no work experience. His sons, who were all fine athletes, had to give up any immediate thoughts of college. Frank was not a wealthy man. The benefit package for a town employee left a lot to be desired, and he had little or no life insurance. I felt as though I had failed because I had never asked Frank to discuss his life insurance needs with me. I should have known better. First of all, a man who had been so interested in my welfare all along would certainly have talked to me, and, knowing Frank, he would probably have bought something just to help *me*.

Second, I had already had a similar experience. Before I tell you about that I want you to know that Frank's wife and kids came out of it OK, but they suffered through some very trying times. A life insurance policy, any life insurance policy, would have been better than no life insurance policy.

Things did not turn out for Frank's family the way he would have wanted. I said "wanted," not needed. Want is a much stronger motivator. While it is true that life insurance can fill the needs of our prospects and clients, it can do much more. It can fulfill the wants of our clients. More agents should talk to people about fulfilling their wants, and not just their needs.

Right after I left the federal Bureau of Narcotics, I went to work in a business with a former narcotic agent friend of mine. He had been a great agent. He worked undercover, as I did, but he was much better at it. He was a very gregarious guy who was accepted by people everywhere. This even carried over to dope peddlers, who are a suspicious lot indeed.

About a year later it became obvious that my friend Pat was in trouble. He was overextended and under-capitalized. That is a common error for businessmen, but I always thought that Pat could overcome it. When I realized that he could barely afford to pay my salary, I decided to look for a different job. I didn't want to be a drain on him or jeopardize my own family's security.

I went into the insurance business on May 2, 1966. Pat asked me to come and talk to him about insurance. He wanted, as he said, "to help me out." I showed him an illustration for $300,000 because he had had a policy for that amount that he had let lapse. He couldn't afford it. He finally agreed to buy a $10,000 whole-life policy with a $25,000 family-income rider. The policy was issued, and the check he gave me bounced! He told me to redeposit. It went through. It was a semian-nual premium of less than $400.

On his 38th birthday, which was New Year's Eve, 1966, he took his wife out to dinner with some friends. He felt ill, went to the men's room, collapsed and was dead on arrival at the hospital with a massive coro-nary. When I delivered the benefit check to his widow, it was all the money she had. Business and personal debts cleaned everything out. The family had to sell their beautiful home in a prestigious Long Island community and move to a totally different atmosphere. Another mother, with no work experience, found a job. Waiting on tables.

I had been in the business less than a year when this happened. I shouldn't have left Frank Sollazzo go without "pestering" him about life insurance. I've never made that mistake again. I hope you don't. *Families survive on life-insurance proceeds.* Scream out the virtues of permanent life insurance. Talk guarantees, not gambles. Is there anyone you haven't asked to buy life insurance because they are friends of yours? Are you still hung up on the "I won't sell to my friends and relatives" trip? Who is more important than your friends and relatives?

Remember the basic truth: Most people don't have any money. That is something you just have to keep repeating to yourself. There are legions of Frank Sollazzos out there for every one rich guy.

The life insurance agent, hammering away at people's resistance, answering objections, putting up with rejection and delay, is doing more to safeguard the lives and lifestyles of families than all the sophisticated investment and "buy term and 'bet' the difference" hot shots put together.

If you are big on investments advice and skeptical about whole life, you may not want to hear this, but most investment is a crap shoot. That doesn't mean you can't do well, or that you shouldn't invest. It means you should invest with dollars you can afford to lose, or at least do without for a while. It means you should follow sound principles like dollar cost averaging. It means you should have a strong cash position first. It means that the family breadwinner's death should not wreak economic havoc on the family. It means you protect incomes against disability before you buy gold coins. It means a safety net. It means *common sense!*

If your experience is anything like mine, you are accustomed to this running battle with certain underwriting types. You'll get a note down on a case saying the client's situation doesn't "justify" so much insurance. What kind of garbage is that? Here is a man or woman wanting to fulfill a dream for their families and maybe generations to come, and some bird sitting at a desk is going to tell them they can't do it. If a client decides he would rather cut down to two restaurant meals a month so he can put more money into his dream, that should be his choice. There is no guidebook on what I should *want* for my family. I don't believe that some underwriter with a calculator and an arbitrary set of financial guidelines ought to dictate what it is I can do for my heirs. Insurance is the only way I can guarantee my dream. I don't want to put that dream at risk.

I remember what Frank Friedler said at the 1986 Million Dollar Round Table: "Risk is unacceptable in providing for my family's financial security." Whole life with guaranteed cash value offers no risk, and many people find that attractive. If your prospects can afford it, they ought to buy it.

Whether the financial planners like it or not, permanent life insurance is the heart and soul of any intelligent and worthwhile plan to fulfill the needs and dreams of our clients and their families. Whole life accumulates cash at decent tax-favored rates of return. It continues to work even during periods of total disability. It becomes a source of low-cost loans to pay off pressing obligations or to seize attractive opportunities. It can guarantee financial security for generations. In case you haven't already read it some-place else, Walt Disney was turned down by the banks he approached with his cartoon character ideas. He borrowed on his life-insurance cash value to start his business. No life insurance, no Mickey Mouse!

There is an important caveat here. Sometimes what your clients want to do or to accomplish either makes no sense or is unreasonable. The following is a true story.

I once sold a Keogh plan (an HR 10) to a man, and, when it came time to discuss his investment vehicles, he told me he had everything all taken care of. I asked him what he was thinking about, and he took me to his basement and showed me his collection of Jim Beam bottles. I thought he was kidding. He wasn't, and I could not change his mind. I never saw him again. He wanted to bet his retirement income on empty whiskey bottles, and he was dead serious!

The point is simple. Many people are misinformed, uninformed or just plain unreasonable when it comes to money and any talk about finances. Our job is to keep them on track and get them to use common sense. If you don't, or they won't, you will never have a client. Even if you sell that person something, it will probably lapse, because he never bought the concept. Like it or not, you are better off walking away.

Family situations are not static. Nor are family dreams. Circumstances change, and as that happens goals change, too. A transfer, a promotion, a new job, an inheritance or an impending birth may necessitate a change in financial plans. There are multiple opportunities for you to help these families, and as you do, the sales will just naturally flow.

The first order of business should always be to provide a safety net. Make sure family members are protected in case of death or disability. Make sure they begin to accumulate a cash reserve. When the first block of the financial planning pyramid is completed you can go on to the next. It's just common sense again! Here is my financial pyramid. There's

---

Financial Pyramid

Remember, there has to be strength as well as balance.

The blocks on the bottom have to be strong to hold the whole thing up.

The blocks on the top are supposed to keep you ahead of the pack.

Only fools spend money on the top of the pyramid before the base is secure.

Risk
Tax shelters
Commodities
Collectibles

Growth
Real estate
Managed stock portfolios
Mutual funds

Savings
Savings accounts
Investment grade life insurance
Government securities
Bonds

Protection
Health insurance
Disability income
Life insurance
Property insurance

nothing tricky about it. As I mentioned earlier, you have to make sure you have a foundation before you build a penthouse. Maybe you think I'm beating a dead horse, but there really are a lot of folks investing in commodities futures who haven't got two weeks' pay in the bank.

This diagram is pretty self-explanatory. I also think it makes an excellent tool for getting your prospects on a common-sense track.

Inflation

When you talk about insuring needs, and dreams and goals beyond needs, you are talking about insuring a little bit of tomorrow. This idea is not always popular, because it means spending more money. However, it make sense, especially for younger families, because they are just starting out and have so many tomorrows ahead of them. Remind them what even modest inflation (say, five percent) can do to buying power and standard of living. If a young wife is 30 and she needs $2,000 a month to live on, remind her that with five percent inflation she will need $4,000 when she is 44 and $8,000 when she is 58, and so on. This may sound like a slippery insurance trick, but it is no trick, baby; that's life.

Another area I'd like to mention at this point is giving advice on those things that are not so readily accomplished. My judo teacher is fond of saying, "No pain, no gain." When you talk to people about their dreams, it has to be understood that certain things are out of reach without sacrifice.

The most common example of this is the desire to buy a home. Unless you are living in the Outback, homes these days are expensive, and lending institutions require sizable down payments. Barring some extraordinary circumstances (like rich and generous parents), accumulating enough cash for a down payment on a home is no easy feat for a young couple.

If you know enough about money, you can certainly give safe advice regarding a savings plan, a sensible yet endurable budget, intelligent secondary borrowing and so on. The main ingredient, however, is still going to be the couple's willingness to sacrifice in the short term to achieve their long-term goal.

I have studiously avoided the use of the phrase *financial planning* because I think it is overused and, frankly, overrated. Nothing I have said so far requires any genius or special education. There are hod carriers who could give you the same advice. It's *common sense*. Some people in the insurance industry don't like to hear that because it strips away the mystique. I love it because it keeps things simple. I don't think an insurance man is in any way diminished if he "only" claims to be a professional in financial common sense.

Disability-Income Insurance

Disability-income (DI) insurance is an area where you can't take no for an answer. Without it, there's a big hole in any safety net. Everything a family has or hopes to have depends on a steady cash flow. A long-term disability could throw a wrench into the best of plans. If both spouses work, both should have permanent, individual, long-term disability insurance. These days folks seem to change jobs more often than they used to, especially younger folks. Therefore, I would put no faith in "the company program."

The next time you get a dumb objection to buying DI, take out a pad and write this in big letters:

W W Y D I Y I S T?

What would you do if your income stopped tomorrow?

Most people you talk to are simply not going to be in a position to go on indefinitely without cash flow. If your prospects have independent unearned income sufficient to their needs, then walk away. They probably couldn't get a company to issue them much DI insurance anyway. Believe me, they are the exceptions. More often than not, the scenario is like the true story that follows.

In 1966, I approached two partners in a restaurant to talk to them about business insurance. I sold them each a life policy equal to their investment and then spoke to them about DI. They finally bought some, but they did not get the top rating. They sometimes worked in the kitchen or on the serving line, so they got the second-best rating.

Some months later I went into the restaurant to eat, and noticed one of my clients sitting at a side table. He didn't look very happy, and I found out why. Working with some of the foods had given him a very unsightly fungus on his hands. He couldn't prepare food or serve it. He had hired someone else to fill in. The restaurant was just getting off the ground, and this was an additional expense he didn't need. Within two weeks he had a check for back benefits, and was paid for a full 24 months. He would tell you today that his business would have failed had he not been able to live on those monthly disability payments. DI—it is just like they say in the credit-card commercials: "Don't leave home without it."

Term Insurance

The smart-money types are always lecturing and writing books about the foolishness of permanent life insurance. Term is always better. No one needs insurance after the kids are grown. Investments always prosper, widows always have enough money and so on. They may as well add that the stork brings mommy a baby.

I have no intrinsic gripe with term. I sell it. I think there are times when it is the only right thing to do. What I do know, however, is that in most situations we encounter, term is not the answer. I sell term to cover short-term business loans. I sell term when a young husband or father needs a lot more protection than he can afford. I sell term when it is not important for it to last a long time. Term is actuarially computed to not be in force when you die. It most likely will not pay estate taxes or be there for your aged widow. It won't do a thing for your dreams of leaving a legacy for your children and grandchildren. Last, when it is compared honestly, it is a lot more expensive than whole life. Sell it where you think it fits, but don't rush into it because someone whines about the whole-life premium.

I have another problem with being too quick to sell term. It is my "stuff" theory. You know what I mean. The amount of stuff a person has tends to accumulate at the same rate as the amount of space he has to store it in.

The same is true of expenses and income. Here's another true story.

I approached a young married man who was my wife's cousin. He had five children and very little coverage. After a review of his financial situation, I realized that he was doing it all with mirrors. I couldn't find enough spare money in his budget to buy insurance even close to what he needed. I focused on his installment debt and discovered that his car payments had four months to go. In four months he would have over $200 a month to spend on protecting his wife and kids. I told him I'd call on him again in four months. I was new in the business and didn't know any better. By the time I got to see him, the "space" in his budget had been filled by other "stuff" (expenses). I should have sold him a policy when I first saw him and put it on interim term for four months. The first payment on the policy could have been deducted from his checking account the month his car payments stopped. Live and learn.

When you have been in the business a while, you learn how to find money in people's budgets. This is always easier when you are talking to a business owner than when you are dealing with salaried people, but there are some things you can do for salaried people, especially if they own a home. Here is one idea that has worked well for me. It's the W-4 form.

Finding Money with the W-4 Form

The W-4 form has helped me find more money for nonbusiness owners than any other vehicle. This is the form that tells your employer the number of exemptions you have, and therefore how much tax should be withheld from your pay. If your exemptions go up, the withholding goes down.

Let's suppose a prospect has $10,000 per year of debt payment that is not tax deductible. If those payments became tax deductible, this prospect would, in the 30 percent tax bracket, pay $3,000 less in taxes. That is a $250 per month increase in disposable income. A remortgage, second mortgage or equity loan on his home could be used to pay off his debts. The payment would now be tax deductible, and he will have "found" $3,000. This is not a method to be used for frivolous reasons, but it is effective in the right situations.

Just in case you think I've lost my mind, I understand that some portion of a mortgage is principal payment and not deductible, but in the early years that is a very small percentage of each payment. The bulk of the payment is interest, and, with the proper kind of debt, most of the payment is deductible.

Feelings Are Often Just As Important As Facts

Of course you have to have the facts of any situation, but if you don't know how your prospects feel about what they are doing or have to do, you may well be on thin ice because they haven't bought the concept. This ties in with talking to people about their *wants* instead of just their needs. People can always figure out how to "make do" with less, thereby reducing their needs. People seldom decrease their wants. When you talk to a man about what he "wants" for his family you are talking to his heart, his emotions, his strongest motivator. You know what you're talking about? That's right! Momma and the kids! Remember, *the theme of almost every sale is momma and the kids.*

One last word about families. When you get past the safety-net stage, be sure you know what you are talking about. If you don't know a good investment from a pie tin, tell them that. Recommend someone else you have confidence in. You will never hurt someone by "knowing" what you don't know!

One thing you should know is that your product, life insurance, is the lifeblood of any successful plan. Without it the plan will almost surely fail. (Even lottery payments run out.) Your product guarantees the plan's completion. It pays for the mortgage, the food bills, the tuition, the new cars, the vacations and the start-up costs of a new business. It can help your kids and their kids buy their first homes. It doesn't go away if the market drops or the yen appreciates.

You've got what everyone wants. Many people don't know it. When you explain the magic properly, they will want it.

Don't be bashful; sell it to them!

Chapter 4

Business Insurance

Talk about things getting romanced to death and surrounded with intrigue, "business insurance" leads the pack! I've talked to agents who have told me that in their companies they sell in the personal market first and then, after about three years, are introduced to the "business" market (whatever that is.) Hopefully, I can take away a lot of the mystique for you.

First of all, businesses are people. When you talk to a business owner about an insurance program, you are usually talking about a program that is going to benefit people. I don't deny that some programs are designed to keep the business afloat should catastrophe strike, but even that is to the benefit of people.

What I'm getting at is very simple. In almost all cases, the fact that distinguishes business insurance from personal insurance is that the premium is paid from the business checkbook. The ultimate beneficiaries of the plan tend to be the families of the business owners. You guessed it, momma and the kids.

I have a lot of clients who own businesses, and therefore you could say I am heavily involved in the business-insurance market. I have never found it particularly complex, and I don't think you will either. In an effort to keep it short and sweet, we won't cover every possible business situation. Let's cover the ones that come up most often.

The Inexpensive Art of Turning Poppa's Business Interest into Cash (Stock Redemption, Cross-Purchase, Trusted Agreement or Whatever Makes You Happy)

You know what this boils down to? Poppa doesn't want his partner's wife as a partner, and he doesn't want momma and the kids dependent on his partner for a living. Believe me, nobody's feelings are hurt because his partner feels exactly the same way. That is true if he has one partner or five partners, and whether he merely tolerates his partner or they are loving brothers. Let me tell you a story.

The "Lump" Beats the Bankers and the Brokers

Don and Vito are partners in a fuel-oil business. They are also brothers. I don't think I've ever met two brothers with a closer relationship. These two guys define brotherly love in the highest sense. I was first referred to them by a pension client of mine who thought these fellows were ready for a pension plan, too. They were, and I put a plan in for their company. Like so many of my fellow Italian-Americans, they were turned off by life insurance and grudgingly allowed me to put a modest amount on each of their lives in the pension plan.

My approach with business owners is to always put first things first. During our initial meeting, I told Don and Vito that, although I'd be delighted to do their pension work, I thought we ought to discuss stock redemption first. I presented all the sound reasons for doing that, but they weren't buying. Their response was just what you would expect. "My brother will take care of my family," "I'm not worried about it," "I trust my brother," and so on. When it was clear to me that I was not getting anywhere, I went ahead and put in the pension plan.

Each anniversary, I went back and placed the updates, and argued the buyout need. Two things became standard. Don and Vito complained about the insurance (they meant the premium), and they stuck to their belief that the surviving brother was all the insurance their families needed. One year they bought some disability insurance, only to drop it the next year. That was a first for me! I'd never had anyone cancel their DI.

Around that time the Congress, in its infinite wisdom, was chipping away at private pensions, and before long Don and Vito agreed to listen to a nonqualified deferred compensation presentation. All the while I kept talking about the growing value of their business and the difficulty of a surviving brother doing justice to his widowed sister-in-law and her children. Nothing happened for quite a while. Then, I guess, lightning struck.

Don called me one day and said he wanted to talk about his business. He and Vito had been discussing what would happen if either died, and he wanted to review their options. I told Don I had a simple solution. He said, "Joe, we don't want to buy any more life insurance. These premiums are killing us." I have to tell you that Don always talks like this because, as my Irish wife says, "You Italians like to cry with a loaf under each arm." After some more conversation, and getting nowhere, I suggested that he speak to an attorney and find out exactly what the consequences of inaction might be.

The following week I brought an attorney to speak to them. He listed the problems and the available courses of action. Insurance was without question the easiest way to accomplish their goals, but they just wouldn't give in. The meeting broke up, with the attorney agreeing to review their wills and their outdated buy-sell agreement. I went back to work.

A week later an agitated Don called me again. "Joe, you got us again! When can you come up and give us an idea what the damn insurance will cost?" I asked him what he was doing that afternoon. A couple of days later, I took applications for one million dollars of whole life on each brother. The combined premium was in excess of $40,000. They also agreed to spend $10,000 each on a deferred-compensation plan funded with L-65. I got the applications and binder checks for all the insurance, arranged the medicals right from their office and left. They had changed their thinking, but I didn't know why. I was about to find out.

I met Don and Vito at the doctor's office, the morning of their physicals. When I arrived, Vito was already in with the doctor, and Don was sitting in the reception area.

"Joe, we did everything we could to avoid buying this insurance. We went to our bank and asked them if they had any ideas. They talked about possible loans and repayment schedules. We went to our stockbroker to see if there was anything he could do. There was nothing."

I had to ask, "So tell me, Don, what made you decide to buy?" His answer was textbook perfection in plain English: "Joe, you're the only guy that can give us the lump."

Do you know how long it takes some people to understand that? I assume that the discussion with the attorney finally conveyed the awesome responsibility a survivor would be faced with, if he had to do it alone. Down deep, Don and Vito always knew it but couldn't bring themselves to pay the premium. They wanted an easier way. There isn't one. They may have thought there was a cheaper way. Sorry, no. They already knew that no one else guaranteed the money.

So the next time somebody runs you around the block when you're trying to sell buyout insurance, paraphrase Don the oil man. Ask, "Who else can give you the lump?" We give 'em the lump, and we do it for pennies on the dollar.

You can make the pill easier to swallow, and I did. For one thing I showed a quick-pay illustration, with no cash payments after the seventh year. Second, since they knew several fuel-oil people who had worked till retirement and then sold their businesses, I pointed out the payout possibilities of the policy's cash value. They still call me every two weeks or so for reaffirmation of what they've done, and the policies are almost two years old!

If you want, you can find someone to discuss a lot of technical points regarding buy-sell with you. I'm sure we could do ten pages just on the alternative minimum tax. If that is your bag, do it. I leave it to the lawyers and accountants. What I do—and you should, too—is make sure the money is where it is supposed to be when it is supposed to be there. In other words, unlike the bankers and the brokers, we give them the lump.

The "Just in Case You Are Hit by a Flaming Oil Truck and Aren't Lucky Enough To Die" Sale

Everyone who has to work for a living should have disability income.

Question to a business owner: Is what you do important around here?

Answer (assuming it's not St. Francis of Assisi):
    "Of course."
Can anyone else do it as well as you?
"Dumb question."
Would business suffer without your expertise, hard
    work and charm?
"What's wrong with you?"

Conversations like this one may not really take place, but you can bet that the average business owner is thinking those thoughts. It is all too often like Carly Simon's song: "Nobody does it better."

When a business owner is disabled, he still needs an income. He doesn't want to deplete his savings. If he is out for a long time, he will probably have to hire someone to do at least some of what he did. If he has a partner, and one of them gets disabled, how long will the one who is working be content to carry 100 percent of the load for 50 percent of the profit?

If your wife's brother is working for you, when do you tell him you can't pay him anymore—before or after he gets out of the hospital?

I don't understand why more DI isn't sold. Most people really cannot afford to go very long without an income. Even in those cases where there is some financial reserve, you would probably still be talking about a change in lifestyle. A fellow in my agency has a tie clasp that reads: "W W Y D I Y I S T?"

What would you do if your income stopped tomorrow? Most people don't even want to think about it. DUMB!

Your income—a continuous satisfactory cash flow —is really your greatest insurance policy. With enough income, you can replace uninsured jewelry, houses and cars that might be lost, burned to the ground or wrecked. Without income, even your property insurance might not be enough. You need income insurance.

For the business owner, this should be a piece of cake. Disability-income insurance premium is a legitimate corporate tax deduction as long as you have a written plan. (You also must be a regular corporation.) The business owner can put in a plan for just one or two employees and it will still qualify.

There are several fine DI carriers to choose from. I suggest you deal with the one that gives you the best service. Most DI companies also will give you a small pocket-sized card that tells you everything you ever wanted to know about the technical and tax aspects of DI policy benefits.

The need for DI is so obvious, I'm not going to talk it to death. I do want to appeal to your enlightened self-interest (you may read "greed"). Consider the effect on your commission income now, and especially in the future. The better DI companies pay renewal commissions of between 10 percent and 15 percent for life, as long as the contract remains in force. If you are a thirty-year-old agent and want to retire early, DI sales will help.

Consider this: If, starting immediately, you commit to sell $30,000 of DI premium a year, in 20 years you will have $600,000 of DI premium on the books. That is between $60,000 and $75,000 per year in renewals just from disability. Start now! This is the only time in this book that I intend to talk in specifics about how much money you, the agent, can make from a sale. The reason is that DI is almost universally needed, and yet it is grossly *undersold*. It is very reasonably priced (especially when you consider the insurance company's extension at risk), and agents still need to be reminded to ask about it. Therefore, I'm appealing to your self interest.

The "Nobody Likes Being Old or Broke but Being Both Is Terrible" Sale (A.K.A. Pensions, Profit Sharing, Deferred Compensation and All That Jazz)

If you have seen a lot of old Jimmy Cagney, George Raft and Humphrey Bogart movies, you probably know about "Sing-Sing." That is the nickname of the New York state correctional facility in Ossining, one of the state prisons. I knew the prison well because my semi-pro baseball team (the Bronx Paramounts) played a lot of doubleheaders there. Those stories could fill another book.

That was the extent of my knowledge about "Sing-Sing" until I was given an orphan policy lead in the spring of 1967 and found myself driving to Ossining. I was on my way to see two brothers who owned a fuel-oil business. (These were the fellows who referred me to Don and Vito of "lump" fame.) I finally found the place. It was a little hole-in-the-wall office attached to a big garage and storage building. The place was a mess. There seemed to be dirt and grease everywhere. The only phone was one that was on the wall, and I was sure I had wasted my day.

They were expecting me. I sat down with the two brothers and began to talk to them about their pension. The agent who sold it to them had left the business, and they wanted service. That's why I was there.

They had a defined benefit plan fully funded with retirement income contracts. I told them I didn't like it and explained split funding. I asked a lot of questions. I wanted to know how they felt about retirement, putting away money for the employees, the importance of tax deductibility, their incomes now and what they thought they would need at retirement. I got the answers I needed, and having spent two or more hours talking with these men, I realized that these two brothers (a) did not agree on much, and (b) did not get along very well.

I found myself working to maintain a balance between the two of them. For a guy whose favorite infantry tactic was Hi Diddle Diddle Right up the Middle, that was not easy. At the end of the day, I walked out of that grimy little office with three applications and a check for $5,000. It was the largest sale I had ever made. I had just been converted to pensions! Over the next 19 years I sold that company several million dollars' worth of insurance. Pension, stock redemption, key-man, DI, the works. More important, the two brothers retired very comfortably on the pension proceeds.

That sale in 1967 gave me a track to run on that I have used ever since. Virtually all my approaches to business owners are pension approaches. As someone has said, "What's not to like?" Consider:

- The deposits are tax-deductible to the company.
- The accumulations are tax-free.
- The deposits are not taxable to the participants.

There is not a lot there to get upset about. Pensions allow people to accumulate large sums of cash with no out-of-pocket outlay. Even if you are not Einstein, you have to like that. I know someone is bound to be thinking, "Sure, but if they didn't put the plan in, the owners would have the money for themselves." That's true, but in most instances I'm dealing with small companies, and the bulk of the deposit is going for the owner. Another point to keep in mind is that most people would not be able to save the same amounts, and certainly not be able to maximize their savings, as much as a plan that accumulates tax-free. This is another one of those areas that a group of technicians could discuss until the millennium. I talk about the benefits, and let the business owner decide. He didn't get to this point because he's stupid.

Sometimes the make-up of the business (number of employees, salaries, ages, etc.) militates against a qualified plan. That is the time to talk about a non-qualified plan. We commonly call this deferred compensation. It can be done with life-insurance contracts like L-65, which will provide all the income. It can be done out of corporate cash flow with life insurance merely guaranteeing the return of the company's money. Either way, you will be hard put to find a business owner or group of executives who are not interested in a little extra money at retirement.

Remember: Nobody likes being old or broke, but being both is the worst!

There are a few other "business" insurance topics which I have chosen not to cover: key-man, group insurance, etc. The reasons are simple. Group insurance is almost an automatic sale, with agents and companies trying to underprice each other out of the business. I have always found it a headache and usually give it to someone else.

True key-man insurance is something I've come across maybe twice in 20 years, so I'm not taking up space with it here. Key-man in the small closely held business is often just a way to get company-paid insurance on the owners. In these situations I use a "bonus" approach. The company pays the premium and charges the executive with income equal to the payment. The company gets a tax deduction for the "bonus." The executive owns the policy for whatever his taxes are on the additional income.

In the bonus illustration in table 4–1, the executive pays taxes of under $5,000 per year for $1 million of insurance (assuming a 28 percent individual tax rate and a 34 percent corporate tax rate). The company pays the premium, but the actual net outlay is lower due to the corporate tax deduction. The executive owns the policy and has access to the cash value, which increases by more than $20,000 per year in the early years and accumulates to more than $1,325,000 in cash at his retirement.

As far as estate planning for business owners, you will find that well-thought-out redemption plans and pensions will go a long way toward solving most estate problems. Estate planning is also· discussed in chapter 6.

TABLE 4–1   Whole Life Executive Bonus Illustration: Variable Loan Rate

Dividends to purchase paid-up additions
Base policy amount: $1,000,000
Annual premium payable: $17,240

Male, Age 40
Nonsmoker

Policy Year	Executive Net After-Tax Outlay	Corporate Net After-Tax Outlay	Total Cash Value	Total Death Benefit
1	$ 4,827	$ 11,378	$ 0	$1,000,000
2	4,827	11,378	20,365	1,013,959
3	4,827	11,378	40,073	1,025,014
4	4,827	11,378	62,079	1,039,271
5	4,827	11,378	84,538	1,056,862
Sum 5	24,136	56,892	84,538	1,056,862
6	4,827	11,378	110,550	1,077,740
7	4,827	11,378	137,339	1,102,188
8	4,827	11,378	167,015	1,130,137
9	4,827	11,378	198,814	1,161,854
10	4,827	11,378	232,950	1,197,493
Sum 10	48,272	113,784	232,950	1,197,493 (age 50)
11	4,827	11,378	270,705	1,237,366
12	4,827	11,378	316,450	1,287,301
13	4,827	11,378	362,985	1,339,869
14	4,827	11,378	413,251	1,397,862
15	4,827	11,378	467,651	1,461,650
Sum 15	72,408	170,676	467,651	1,461,650
16	4,827	11,378	527,604	1,531,623
17	4,827	11,378	592,413	1,607,840
18	4,827	11,378	662,404	1,690,446
19	4,827	11,378	737,991	1,779,723
20	4,827	11,378	819,606	1,875,980
Sum 20	96,544	227,568	819,606	1,875,980
Sum 25	120,680	284,460	1,325,577	2,461,862 (age 65)

NOTE: Amounts not shown as guaranteed are based on our current interest-sensitive dividend scale and are neither guaranteed nor estimates for the future. This proposal is not a contract and is subject to the contract provisions that are stated in the policy.
SOURCE: Phoenix Mutual Life Insurance Company.

Keep to the basics. Give your clients "the lump." Make sure they are *not* old and broke. Make sure they have an income in case they get hit by a flaming oil truck and don't die. Do that, and you'll have no trouble with business insurance.

Chapter 5

Financial Planning

As far as I am concerned, I've heard enough about financial planning. As George Burns is fond of saying, "It's been done." Whenever I read an article or hear a speaker on the subject I think of something that happened before I ever thought about a life-insurance career.

A close friend of mine and his wife were about to have their third child, and money was really tight. Although they were very careful about their expenditures and he made a respectable income, there never seemed to be an extra dime in the house.

In search of a solution, they asked a CPA friend of theirs to come to their home one evening and see if he could help. I happened to be there. This fellow was very sincere and intent on doing a good job. He studied tax returns, rifled through receipts and billing statements, and generally immersed himself in the financial data of my friends. They were very hopeful because this fellow, in addition to being a CPA, was a senior officer at a major New York bank.

After about two hours, the man took off his glasses, put all the forms and statements back into their proper places, and looked up at my two friends. He sighed and said, "Jack . . . Peggy . . . you have a basic inability to accumulate funds!" We all looked at him as if he were from Mars. We knew that! These people wanted to know why, and what they could do about it. Jack and Peggy either had to make more money, or spend less. Peggy could have gone to work, but with two kids under six and another about to arrive, that was not really a viable solution. Jack was salaried and not in a position to demand exponential leaps in income. Cutting expenses or increasing disposable income were the only real possibilities. They managed to do that on their own (with no help from me—I was still a narcotic agent). They bought a house, revised their W-4 and paid less taxes with approximately the same monthly expense. Voilà! More money!

Some people are very fond of creating and perpetuating a mystique about financial planning. Don't get caught up in it. There are only a few generic problems and there are only a few generic answers. Consider the following:

- People don't have enough money.
- People have a lot of money and want to preserve it for their heirs.

- People don't protect their incomes.
- People have no will or the wrong will.
- Property is not titled correctly.

Most problems revolving around family income, taxation, conservation and the like can be placed into one of the above categories.

Financial problems and solutions affected by legislation often require technical knowledge and/or legal assistance. I don't believe this should get in the way of the basic solution. Situations are most often a lot simpler than the so-called experts would have you believe.

The purpose of the book is to take the mystique out of insurance planning. It is not to impress you with a recitation of internal revenue codes and technical jargon.

If you are going to do some planning for people, it has to be *their* plan. They have to know what they are trying to do. You, hopefully, are going to give them some ideas on how to do it. It doesn't make a lot of difference whether you are securing basic protection for family income or recommending a trust to avoid estate taxes or whatever. It has to accomplish their goal, make sense, and they have to be willing to do it.

What we do IS, and after all should be, *common sense.*

Chapter 6

Estate Planning

When I first came into the insurance business, the predominant theme of the training program was estate planning. Wow! It was exciting. Here I was, a liberal arts graduate of a small Jesuit college, learning about trusts, wills, community property and the like. This was a far cry from my six years of Latin and my college Greek courses. It was light years away from my English major and the endless philosophy courses in the Jesuit Ratio Studiorum. I was going to be an "estate planner."

There seemed to be such mystery and intrigue to it. The government "bad guys" were trying to swallow up a good part of what a man had worked all his life to leave to his heirs, and we were devising ways and means to keep it all together. We were the "good guys!" It was great.

As time went on, I found myself involved in long conferences concerning tax law and trusts and wills. I was occasionally upset by the fact that these conferences often tended to go right past the answer and rehash this or that issue or bring up some obscure point which had questionable relevance.

It wasn't long before I had no patience for these talkathons. They just weren't my style. When you have all the information you need, you can figure out what the real problems are and then come up with the best way to solve them. There are only a few basic problems in planning people's finances and just a handful of generic answers. (See "Estate Questions" in the Appendix of this book.) I didn't come to this conclusion last week. I've felt this way a long time.

Over the years, there have been many changes in the estate tax law. Some have helped, and some have hurt; but nothing has altered the nature of the problems that can arise, or has led to radically different solutions. The answers are still the same as they were 20 years ago: a new or different will, a trust of one kind or another, a gift program, life insurance outside the estate to pay the taxes and so on.

Sure, there have been new ideas in trust work, but it is still a trust; and wills may be written differently now, but they are still wills. Life insurance is a lot cheaper than it was 20 years ago, but it still does the same job. Twenty years ago people were talking about private annuities and they are still a good idea.

Unfortunately, what has not changed is the propensity of some people to romance these things to death. Some folks just love to create and perpetuate a certain mystique about getting the estate-planning job done. That is just not my schtick. After all, what we are doing is conserving the money for momma and the kids. There is no mystery about that.

I don't classify categories of wealth because it's a matter of orientation. What is "super-rich" to one person may be "comfortable" to another. To each his own. I'm not overly concerned about different people's criteria, as long as what they are saying is within reason. I had a young builder tell me early in his career that his wife could "get by" on $300 per month. He was making about ten times that! He was being unreasonable, and I told him so. He didn't agree. I walked out. That was in 1966. Today the same fellow is approaching $2 million of insurance for his wife and kids. He has never told me what changed his thinking, but I'm glad he did. He now makes about $200,000 a year, and his insurance at seven percent will leave his wife with plenty of income, even with some unforeseen inflation. He started out being unreasonable, and it just wasn't something I wanted to deal with. Today he is one of the most responsible husbands and fathers I know. Oh, yes, he bought the insurance from me.

All estate-planning situations are not created equal, even if the estates are. Here are a couple of examples.

If Income Is Not a Problem

Say you are merely trying to keep a client's estate intact, out of the clutches of the government. We want to minimize the bite of estate taxes. You can put some of the property in trust, for example, or you can begin a gift program (if it makes sense). What I mean by that is that sometimes the size of the estate is so large that it will grow faster than it can be given away. A person with an $8 million estate, growing at ten percent per year, would have to give away $800,000 each year just to stay even! Talk about Merry Christmas!

What you probably would try to do in this instance is freeze the estate value wherever possible, and provide some insurance proceeds outside the estate to cover a portion or all of the tax. I'm sure there are a number of brilliant ideas out there for this situation. Maybe I could even discuss them for hours at a time, if I had nothing else to do. But . . . what I do in these cases is what I do when my wife tells me the oil burner isn't working: I call the "oil burnerologist." I call one of several good attorneys I know who specialize in estate planning. Their answers are seldom much different from the ones a good life-insurance agent would give. They just do the necessary documents. We don't do documents because we don't practice law.

We sell discounted dollars to pay the tax! To the best of my knowledge, no one has come up with a better or cheaper way to pay the estate-tax bill. Remember, that is our business. We sell money!

Isn't that what it is all about? Keep the taxable estate as low as you reasonably can, pass as much of the estate as possible to the people it is intended for, and pay whatever taxes you must pay with the cheapest dollars you can find.

That doesn't have to be complicated. You don't need an endless round of meetings. And you certainly don't have to surround the whole matter with a mystique that is not called for.

Take the example we just used (an $8 million estate). Maybe you can transfer some assets; maybe you can make gifts of some assets; maybe you can sell some assets for a life annuity; and maybe, if a person's business interest comprises a large portion of his estate, you can recapitalize and freeze the value of his stock. Whatever you do, chances are good that in most cases there are still going to be taxes to pay, and life insurance will be the best way to pay them. Let me say it again: That's the essence of the job in this situation—to minimize the tax bite and find the cheapest way to pay it.

Let me comment briefly on a couple of the tactics I've mentioned.

Gifts

A gift program doesn't take a lot of explanation. Just be sure that when your clients are in gift-tax-paying situations, they are not paying more in taxes than they would have to pay in premiums if they just kept the property and planned to pay the estate tax.

A Life Annuity

This is very simple. An older person with assets worth, say, $2 million sells those assets to others in exchange for a life annuity. This is calculated just like a regular nonrefundable life annuity. The persons (usually children) who bought the assets pay out a monthly income for life. At the annuitant's death, no further payments are due. The deceased's estate does not include the "sold" property.

I have dealt with estates of $8 million and estates of $48 million, and my experience is that the kind of people who amass these fortunes are not the kind of people who are easily convinced to give up control. While the answers may look perfect on your presentation easel, you're in for a serious jolt of reality when you ask your prospect to do some of the things required by your technically perfect answers. As I've said elsewhere, feelings are as important as facts. So make sure your client is amenable before you recommend. Now let's look at another situation.

When Income Is a Problem

In this situation you are talking about either inadequate liquidity in an otherwise sizable estate, or an estate of insufficient size to provide adequate income. Either way, you have to liquefy the estate so momma and the kids will have an income. Insurance always plays a part in these cases. Here's an exaggerated example:

An estate comprises a small amount of liquid assets and 4,000 acres of unimproved property worth $1,000 per acre. Those 4,000 acres may be salable or they may not. Even if they are salable, there will probably be a capital gains (income) tax to pay. Add to that the fact that "widow" sales seldom attract fair market value, and you can see that it might be just as easy, and perhaps even cheaper, to buy a bunch of life insurance. Then momma and the kids will have plenty of cash and be able to deal with the property at their own pace while exploring their options. They will be in a less economically stressed position and able to think more clearly. As someone said, "It's hard to see the handwriting on the wall when your back is up against it."

Earlier I referred to the use of attorneys. Whether you are comfortable dealing with attorneys or not, they are a necessary part of estate work. A fair number of attorneys out there are very knowledgeable in this area, and you would be well advised to find one with whom you have some chemistry and build a relationship. I have been very fortunate in this regard.

When I came into the insurance business in 1966, the advanced underwriting manager in the agency was an attorney named Don Young. We got along quite well; but, as often happens in our business, he left to go with someone else, and I joined the company I've now been with for 19 years (Phoenix Mutual). When Don and I met up again a few years later, he was heading up his own small firm, which specialized in estate and pension plannning. I resumed a business and personal relationship with Don. Although his firm has grown substantially over the years, its major component is still estate and pension planning. I have learned a great deal from Don and his associates since then. Nothing, however, has been more beneficial to me than their reinforcement of my style and philosophy. They *do not* maintain a mystique. They *do not* complicate. They keep things clear and simple.

I have seen Don Young deal with estates of $25 million and more, while analyzing the problems and prescribing the solutions on one or two pages of a yellow pad. He quickly finds out what clients have and what the estate is worth. Then he finds out how they feel about their situation and tells them very clearly what their options are. It hardly ever takes him a long time to do this, and I have never had a client who left Don's office confused.

There is no doubt that other advisers can be an obstacle. They can get in the way of the solution and contribute to the problem. Sometimes it is just plain ignorance; sometimes it is jealousy born out of territorial protection. When that happens, you have to be bold. Naturally, I have a story to illustrate what I mean. This is my favorite experience in the insurance business for two reasons: (1) It wasn't my case (I was helping one of my agents), and (2) it generated over $400,000 in life-insurance premium for a very loyal and hard-working salesman who deserved it.

Nat King Cole Sings "La Bamba"

An agent in my agency, whom I'll call Bob Marine, had been working for some time on developing an estate-planning case for the owners of a very large, international, privately owned food company. Progress was slow, but reasonably steady. Bob approached me one day and asked if I would help him with the case. I was delighted to help because (a) that is what I'm there for, and (b) it demonstrated that a strong producer in the agency's established organization had confidence in me.

On our first visit to the prospect it became evident that he and I had a certain favorable chemistry. We both came from immigrant ethnic families, we shared the same values, and we both spoke his native language. On that first visit, we agreed that there was a problem, explored various options available to solve the problem and agreed that life insurance was an important part of the solution.

Subsequent meetings resulted in a comparison of other insurance products and an agreement that, no matter what, the man who deserved the business was the man who did the work, Bob Marine. Eventually the client agreed that Phoenix Mutual's survivorship-whole-life policy was the right product. He filled out an application and agreed to be examined. Before he would give us a binder check, however, he insisted that he had to meet with his attorney and accountant. Bob and I said that would be fine, but that we would like to be there. It was all arranged.

The law firm was one of the biggest and most prestigious in New York City. The accountant arrived before we did and was also no lightweight. Everyone exchanged pleasantries, and we began to discuss the client's situation. One of the recommendations was recapitalization to freeze an already very large estate, and the other main ingredient was a $10 million survivorship-life plan. The attorney and the accountant each had a few words of wisdom about the recap and then began to question Bob about the policy and other alternatives. It became obvious after a while that they either didn't know what they were talking about or simply wanted to make the decision about where the business went. They came up with a lot of reasons why the client should delay action.

After a while I'd had enough, so I stood up and said to the client, whom I'll call Jim, "Jim, you see this guy? [I pointed to the attorney.] The longer he takes, the more he makes. You see that guy? [I pointed to the accountant.] The longer he takes, the more he makes. You see Bob here? He is going to do just fine no matter how long these other guys delay. Me? I'm along for the ride, and to help Bob out if I can, but I'm not the salesman on this case. There is only one sure loser here, Jim, and that is you. I sure don't want any more Nat King Coles around here."

With that, the attorney and accountant, both of whom had turned beet-red and had never looked up from their proposals, turned toward me with quizzical looks on their faces. The client was also confused. "Joe, what do you mean, Nat King Cole?"

I briefly recounted the story about how Nat Cole had applied for a life-insurance policy while appearing in Las Vegas. He didn't bind it because his advisers were trying to decide ownership, payment schedules and so on. When the agent finally came around to deliver the policy, Nat Cole's cancer had already been discovered and the agent had to send the policy back. Nat Cole died about six months later, and the estate had to borrow $1 million to pay the estate tax. Natalie Cole became a singer to earn money to pay off that debt.

Then I turned to Jim, the client, and said, "I guarantee you, my friend, that nobody in your family is going to make $10 million singing "La Bamba!"

Jim said, "You know something, I always liked that song, but I never knew the words." Hey, what else could I do? I got to my feet, 35 stories above Park Avenue, and I sang "La Bamba!"

The lawyer and accountant were thoroughly defused. In a couple of days, Bob Marine had a binder check of $40,000. He placed that case and led the agency for the year! The recapitalization hasn't been done to this day that I know of, and the life insurance trust took eight months. Thank God for Nat Cole and "La Bamba."

There is a second part to this, and that was Jim's brother, who was a lot less affable. He ran the other part of the family business, which was 2,000 miles away. After a discussion with Jim, it was agreed that, for the plan to be complete, his brother should do the same thing. Arrangements were made, and Bob and I flew out to see Jim's brother and partner. The brother kept us waiting for an hour and was rude, insulting and a know-it-all. Bob was embarrassed at having me sit through this, and I felt sorry for Bob and was furious at the man in front of me. Never having been accused of an excess of patience, I finally got up and said, "Bob, I'm leaving. I'll wait for you outside. If I stay here much longer, I'm going to knock this guy out." I left. Bob came out about 20 minutes later and wasn't very happy—with me or the situation. I told him that no sale, even one with $200,000 in premium, was worth groveling for. The man owed us some respect, and we weren't getting it.

When we got back to New York, we met with the first brother, Jim. I told him what happened and how I felt about it. He was truly dismayed and apologized for his brother's behavior. Several months later Jim flew out to "speak" to his brother, and when he came back he called and said, "Go out to see my brother. He is ready to buy." Bob went, and sold his second $10 million policy. The guy was sweet as pie.

Each of these brothers had several sons. Neither brother wanted his family's interest in the company diminished. They didn't want their stock "retired" or sold out to the surviving brother. They didn't want stock sold to outsiders, and they didn't want the government confiscating what their parents and they had worked 50 years to put together. They paid the price to pay the tax!

There wasn't any mystery. There was a problem, and only a few things that could be done. We reviewed the options, put together a reasonable solution and sold it. The clients' wishes were fulfilled, and the tax is going to get paid, at pennies on the dollar. When either brother dies, everything will stay in place for momma and the kids.

Here is the contract we used to provide the $10 million coverage. It is survivorship whole life. The death benefit is paid at the death of the second to die.

The illustrations you see are not sophisticated; that is intentional. You have a "quick-pay," showing only seven and a half years of premium payments in a standard policy, and a second illustration showing eight premium payments using a term component for part of the death benefit (Phoenix Mutual's Option Term).

The illustrations in tables 6–1 and 6–2 use $1 million for purposes of simplicity. Separate million-dollar policies on each life would have a combined premium of $62,300, so you can see the savings inherent in the survivorship policy.

Estate-planning problems haven't changed much in 22 years. People still want to accomplish the same things, are faced with the same obstacles, and use the same generic solutions. You still almost always need an attorney, and life insurance is still the cheapest and surest way to pay the tax. Amen.

TABLE 6–1   Survivorship Whole Life Illustration: Variable Loan Rate

Proceeds payable at second death			Male, Age 55
Annual premiums payable to second death: $20,840			Nonsmoker
Dividends to purchase paid-up additions			Female, Age 55
			Nonsmoker

Policy Year	Annual Premium Payable in Cash	Total Cash Value	Total Death Benefit
1	$ 20,840	$ 0	$1,000,000
2	20,840	25,789	1,018,352
3	20,840	50,090	1,033,871
4	20,840	77,241	1,053,696
5	20,840	106,445	1,077,903
Sum 5	104,200	106,445	1,077,903
6	20,840	138,922	1,106,588
7	14,012	166,463	1,103,235
8	0	181,763	1,080,632
9	0	196,951	1,061,729
10	0	214,132	1,046,487
Sum 10	139,052	214,132	1,046,487 (age 65)
11	0	233,415	1,034,844
12	0	252,938	1,026,762
13	0	273,840	1,022,238
14	0	297,310	1,021,826
15	0	322,543	1,026,345
Sum 15	139,052	322,543	1,026,345
16	0	353,240	1,039,024
17	0	384,803	1,053,085
18	0	418,682	1,070,805
19	0	454,059	1,092,236
20	0	492,021	1,117,237
Sum 20	139,052	492,021	1,117,237 (age 75)

NOTE: Amounts not shown as guaranteed are based on our current interest-sensitive dividend scale and are neither guaranteed nor estimates for the future. This proposal is not a contract and is subject to the contract provisions that are stated in the policy.
SOURCE: Phoenix Mutual Life Insurance Company.

TABLE 6–2 Survivorship Whole Life Illustration with Option Terms: Variable Loan Rate

Proceeds payable at second death Male, Age 55
Annual premiums payable to second death: $14,891 Nonsmoker
Dividends to buy term insurance with any balance Female, Age 55
 to purchase paid-up additions Nonsmoker

Policy Year	Annual Premium Payable in Cash	Total Cash Value	Total Death Benefit
1	$ 14,891	$ 0	$1,000,000
2	14,891	17,885	1,007,202
3	14,891	34,614	1,009,226
4	14,891	53,234	1,012,011
5	14,891	73,159	1,014,841
Sum 5	74,457	73,159	1,014,841
6	14,891	95,242	1,017,725
7	14,891	118,936	1,020,719
8	11,558	141,480	1,023,298
9	0	152,306	1,024,332
10	0	164,463	1,025,378
Sum 10	115,798	164,463	1,025,378 (age 65)
11	0	178,026	1,026,458
12	0	191,648	1,027,580
13	0	206,129	1,028,751
14	0	222,302	1,030,025
15	0	239,274	1,031,405
Sum 15	115,798	239,574	1,031,405
16	0	260,560	1,036,099
17	0	281,968	1,039,191
18	0	304,782	1,042,243
19	0	328,376	1,045,337
20	0	353,501	1,048,343
Sum 20	115,798	353,501	1,048,343 (age 75)

NOTE: Amounts not shown as guaranteed are based on our current interest-sensitive dividend scale and are neither guaranteed nor estimates for the future. This proposal is not a contract and is subject to the contract provisions that are stated in the policy.
SOURCE: Phoenix Mutual Life Insurance Company.

Chapter 7

The Quadrant

When I came into the life-insurance business. I was taught the "funnel" talk. A man named Stu Smith invented it many years ago. It is a fine approach talk, and I've given it a thousand times. If you are not familiar with it, look at Tom Wolff's Capital Needs Analysis talk, which is essentially the same thing. Tom was smart enough to change it a little and copyright it. God bless him.

In my constant search for simplification, I found myself cutting the talk shorter and shorter. Finally, it made sense to just develop my own track to run on. I call it the quadrant.

Simple Financial Common Sense	
Investments	Other
Cash	Insurance A) Life: B) Disability:

I draw this little quadrant and write the words you see above. Then I begin asking questions. "How are you fixed for cash?" When I get an answer, I write it down. Then I ask how my client feels about it, and why. A fact question, and a feeling question. "How do you feel about your cash reserve?" Whatever answer I get, I write down in the "Cash" section and ask another question: "Why?" When you get that answer, write it down. Now your quadrant looks like this:

Investments	Other
Cash $4,000 Not thrilled with it. Won't cover emergencies.	Insurance A) Life: B) Disability:

Do the same thing in the next box, "Insurance." "How much personally owned life insurance do you have? How do you feel about it? Why?" I have to tell you that this is the most amazing sequence. Nine times out of ten, when I ask how much life insurance a person has, I get an answer something like this: "You are probably going to say I need more, and you are probably right." Wow! Sign here.

Then I ask about "Insurance (B)"—disability-income insurance. "How much DI do you have?" Most people have none! The next question is, "Why not?" Now you have to make this point: "People between the ages of 20 and 50 are more likely to get disabled than die." People insure houses, cars, boats, savings deposits, yet fail to insure the one asset that allows them to have all the others—their income! No one should walk around without disability-income insurance. Answer the questions and get some feelings and reasons for the feelings, and write them down under "Insurance (B)."

When I get to the "Investments" section. I ask the same questions but also why the man has the investments he has, and what his objective is or was in selecting those investments. You want to make sure his vehicle will get him where he wants to go.

In the "Other" box, I'll find out about unimproved land, for instance, or a summer home, a condo, inheritance and so on.

For a summary of all this, see the Appendix.

Try to get inside the mind and heart of your prospect. Remember, people do things for *their* reasons, not ours. When you are all done, the basic quadrant might look like this:

Investments		Other
Stocks	$0	Employer:
Bonds	$0	$25,000 group term
Mutual fund	$2,000	Major medical
IRA	$0	Blue Cross
Real estate	$0	Inheritance $0
Cash		**Insurance**
$4,000		A) Life: $50,000 whole life.
		Probably need more.
Not thrilled with it.		
Won't cover emergencies.		B) Disability: None.
		Never thought about it.

When you add all this up, you have $6,000 in liquid assets, $50,000 of life insurance, no disability insurance and a standard employment benefit package. I take stock of what the client has just told me and recount for him what he has that is liquid and what isn't, what is guaranteed and what isn't.

Then I'll ask what he wants to accomplish for himself and his family. I want to find out what his personal goals, aspirations, and dreams are for himself, his family (if he has one), his later years, his work.

Not all of this is absolutely germane to a financial plan, but it is very critical in finding out what your prospect thinks is important right now. Over the years, as you visit with your client, the answers will change and there will be new priorities. That is why you have to have periodic reviews.

Let's suppose your prospect is single. He may be interested in saving a little more money, buying a new car, getting a better apartment or finding a better job. Write these things down. Talk to this person. Share his interests and dreams.

You can talk to him about a systematic savings plan that kills two birds with one stone—life 65, which provides cash accumulation and an increasing death benefit. You can talk to him about cars and remind him that he always has to have the money to make payments, and so he needs disability-income insurance.

You can explain that investing should be done with discretionary income. He should build his guarantees first—cash and insurance. Be confident, be firm, make sense and try to satisfy the prospect's wants as well as his needs. But remember, needs come first. That is common sense.

When I get those answers, I draw another quadrant. This one is closer to a "T" account, for those of you who have taken an accounting course. I put the assets on one side and the objectives on the other side:

Assets	Objectives
$4,000 Cash	$15,000 Cash
$50,000 Life insurance	New car
$2,000 Mutual fund	

I put what he has in assets on the left side of the quadrant, and a dollar cost for what he wants to do on the right side of the quadrant. From there, it's simple.

If there is not enough money to do what the guy wants, you have to create some. If there is enough money, you check out the inflation possibilities. If there is more than enough money, you are in an estate-planning situation.

If you are talking to a business owner, the questions are the same. (See "Business Questions" in the Appendix.) The answers tend to revolve around the business, and so do the solutions. The kind of things you want to cover in a business or estate-planning situation are covered in chapters 4 and 6. The major points to keep in mind are basic. For example, a business owner probably considers his business his biggest investment. Your job is to make sure it is liquid, even if he is not there. A business owner can accumulate large amounts of cash, stocks, bonds and so on through a pension plan. As you know, pension plans are doubly effective because they are on a pretax basis. Simply stated, a business owner's business can supply not only his safety net but the stuff his dreams are made of.

As you go through each part of the quadrant with the business owner, be sure you ask the questions not only with regard to his personal accounts, but also in light of what his business is or could be providing for him—for instance, all of those benefits a man would like for himself and his family.

The quadrant is simple to draw, easy to remember, and the questions are always the same: How much? How do you feel? Why? After that, you find out what the prospect wants to do, and help him do it. Remember, there are only a handful of generic problems, and about as many answers.

Life insurance plays a big part in anybody's game plan, and that is what you provide. Let me finish with the greatest secret of all:

YOU MUST KNOW WHAT YOU KNOW.

If there is any one thing that explains the success of great insurance salesmen, it is that. They know what they know. They are not deterred. Whether the prospect wants to hear it or not, they tell him that he must have guarantees, that he cannot risk his family's security, that the business won't just "work it out." In other words, that in so many situations they have the only answer. Life insurance!

Keep the basic truths in mind. Don't get fooled by all the bull. There is no mystery after all. It is just for momma and the kids.

Chapter 8

The New Agent

I have been an agency manager for 19 years. I have started two fairly scratch agencies, and in a short time both were leaders in the company's new organization ratings. New agents are the lifeblood of the industry, and, if we don't keep bringing them through, the industry will suffer and possibly die. This chapter is addressed to the new agent. It is sort of a one-way conversation. I hope you all listen.

The first thing to keep in mind is that you are in business for yourself. You may have heard that this is the last bastion of free enterprise. That is not true. There are many free-enterprise opportunities around. What makes this business so special is that it requires a minimum capital investment, and you can make a ton of money. Remember, it is your business. You are responsible for your success, and you will have only yourself to blame for your failure. If you are told to do something and don't, if you are asked to learn something and don't, then the results of that inaction are your responsibility.

It really makes no difference whether you are running a Burger King or a franchise wallpaper store, you have to do those things that successful people do or you won't succeed.

I guess you have heard a lot of conflicting stories and opinions about being a life-insurance agent. Some of your friends probably think you're crazy. Your mom has probably told you that all your friends already have insurance. If your dad is like mine, he may be telling you it is not too late to get a good job in a corporate management training program. If you are an older new agent who has already had a career someplace else, you may be getting more subtle reactions of the same nature. Don't worry about it. If everyone knew what a great business this is, there would be too many people in it and that many fewer people to sell to.

Unless this is the first chapter you've read, you know what I think the essence of this business is. I'll say it again. We put the money that people need, right where it is needed, at the precise time it is needed. Now in terms of doing something important, it doesn't get much more important than that; and in terms of helping people, it doesn't get much better than that. The training program you receive in your company or agency should tell you how to go about building your business. Some do it better than others. Let me tell you what I have told my own son about getting started.

The Really Basic Basics

After you have completed your licensing requirements, be sure you understand your company's products. It isn't necessary to know every little thing the company sells, but you should have a good grasp of those products you are likely to be using most of the time, and a familiarity with the rest of the portfolio. You may be thinking I shouldn't have wasted your time saying that, because it's a truism. I wish it were. I have met an awful lot of agents who have been in this business a lot longer than I, who had absolutely no understanding of some of our strongest products. I've spent hours explaining the workings of a life paid-at-65 policy to an agent who is regularly among the company's leaders. It scares you sometimes!

Don't get the impression that I expect you to be an actuary. Not at all. I do think you have to know when certain contracts fit a situation better than others. I do think you have to know the applicability and suitability of the various dividend options. In other words, you have to know what products make sense for the client and situation. Clients are not always comfortable with the product best suited for their situation. You have to know your client's feelings as well as your products.

Another basic basic you need is a simple approach talk. Maybe it isn't a talk at all, but simply a thought or an idea to get a person's attention, to arouse their interest and so on. You may make it as sophisticated or simple as you like, as long as you are comfortable with it. In chapter 7 you will find the talk I'm using these days and that I'm teaching new agents. It is called "The Common-Sense Quadrant." Maybe your agency or company teaches a different approach or sales talk. Use whatever suits you best.

The most basic of all basics, I've left for last. It is self-discipline. It may be trite to say, "Plan your work and work your plan," but too many agents regularly allow themselves to be distracted. Sure it is more fun to talk about last night's ball game or Sunday's golf game, but there is a time and place for that and it's seldom the same time as prospecting, studying, preparing or presenting. In the next few chapters we'll cover some of these basics in more detail. I must confess I have difficulty going into detail about something that is supposed to be basic. After all, if it is so basic, what am I going into detail about? Well, some folks are funny, and I guess if something is too simple it is somehow suspect.

Doing What You Have To Do

In 30 years of studying the Japanese martial arts, I have learned that dogged application and repetition will make certain actions reflexive after a while. And so it is that after blocking thousands of punches thrown at your face, which you knew were coming, you automatically block a punch when you were not forewarned.

Another valuable lesson from those years of study is the need to focus. It is the focusing of all your energies on a single point that exponentially increases the power of your technique. It is why mere mortals can break two-inch boards. It is also why anorexic-looking professional golfers can hit a five iron 200 yards, while the rest of us can only shake our heads in wonder and applaud.

These lessons are very applicable in the insurance business as well. The person who only talks to two or three people a week about insurance will not handle the give and take of a closing discussion as well as someone who has regularly spoken to 15 people a week. The agent who has received and responded to thousands of objections and excuses will handle them infinitely better than the agent who has not.

What all this is obviously leading up to is that a new agent must generate a lot of activity. He (or she) must focus on that as his primary goal. He must understand that the first order of business is finding people who will listen to your story. Given the very basic basics, you *must* find people to talk to. Every agent and general agent, manager and home-office trainer in the world has his own pet method. Someone once said, perhaps correctly, that any prospecting method will work as long as you *DO* it. While that may be technically true, it doesn't work for me on a practical basis. There are some prospecting methods I dislike so much that if I *had* to use them, I'd find another line of work.

I like to break all prospecting down into two categories: the easy way, and the hard way. Strangely enough, I prefer the easy way.

The easy way is talking to people you know.

Everything else is the hard way!

Included under the easy way is talking to people who are friends of people you know. These are referrals.

If you had your choice of a friendly reception or a hostile one, would you really choose the hostile one?

If you had your choice of talking with people with whom you had something in common or people who were a blank to you, would you really choose the blanks?

I guess you have seen the commercials on TV about hamburger A (the hot, delicious hamburger) or hamburger B (the cold, dry hamburger), right? Well remember, it is just as absurd in real life to choose hamburger B, but people do it every day when they decide to prospect the hard way.

Now is the time when you can hear the little gremlin in your head saying, "I don't want to have to call on my friends and relatives." Let's deal with that right away. If you are in this business on a lark, or while you are looking for a "better job," you are right. Don't bother your friends and relatives. They might buy something thinking that you would be there to take care of their needs for a long time. If you are here "until something comes up," let them become involved with a career insurance agent who will take care of their needs.

But if you are committed to a career in this great profession, then who would you rather have serving the people you care about—you, or someone cold, unknown, a stranger? That's right! *You! Hamburger A!*

Take the Pressure Off

One of the problems with calling on friends and relatives is the pressure, real or perceived, that you feel when asking your friends to listen to what you have to say. If you could remove that tension, not only from yourself but from the people you are calling on, you would probably get off to a much faster start. Let me outline some simple steps to take the pressure off, get the appointments and make some solid early sales.

1. Make a list of everybody you know that you have a friendly relationship with. This will range from family and close personal friends to casual but friendly acquaintances.

2. Now separate the list into three categories; (a) very close friends and relatives, (b) good friends, (c) everyone else.

3. Decide which end of the list you want to begin calling first. There are two schools of thought: (a) First call the people you're closest to because you care about them the most and they should be the most considerate; or (b) First call the casual acquaintances because they'll probably agree to see you, and, if you make a mistake with them or lose the sale, it won't make as much difference.

Personally, I prefer calling on people I'm closest to precisely because they will be more considerate. It's always nice to have a few successes under your belt when you get down to the tougher situations.

OK, you have your list, you've decided whom you're going to call first and you are ready to call. Now you freeze up. You are terrified. You sit there saying to yourself, "What the hell am I going to say?" Here are a couple of suggestions. Some of our new agents have used them, or some variation of them, with pretty good results.

"Hi, Charlie, this is Joe. Are you sitting down? OK, I'm calling to tell you I've decided on a career in the insurance business. Don't panic, I just want the opportunity to get your reaction to the kind of work I'm doing and will be trained to do in the future. When would be a good time to get together?"

Or, you can try this . . .

"Hi, Pat, this is Joe Casale. Pat, I've just made a career change. I've gone into the insurance business, and I'm really excited about the opportunities available to me. I'd like to show you the kind of work that I do and get your reaction to it. Don't worry, I'm not going to force you to buy anything. In fact, I'll leave all my official papers in the car. When would be a good time to get together?"

Hopefully, these two examples will give you the idea. You want your friend to understand that this is going to be a nonthreatening interview.

These techniques, or some variation of them, work. I know because they worked for me over 20 years ago. When I came into the insurance business, most of the people I knew were federal narcotic agents. I had just left the Bureau of Narcotics prior to coming into this business, and narcotic agents, like most law-enforcement types, are a very close-knit group who tend to socialize only with each other. Besides, most of the other people I knew were in jail, and I had put them there!

When my first manager asked me to write down a list of prospects, the best I could do was 12 names. Amazingly enough, they hired me anyway. Well, I used the exact technique described above. I told people I wasn't even going to bring a pen to the meeting, just a pad and pencil so I could describe the kind of work I was doing.

Several of those "nonprospects" bought from me, and, to a man, they gave me referrals. One of the most interesting things was that even an agent with whom I hadn't been so friendly bought from me because he had heard about the kind of work I was doing and felt he and his family would benefit from it.

An agent I hired a couple of years ago called on his sister and her husband first. He sold them, and then took her address and phone book and asked about each person in there as he copied the names and phone numbers. To the best of my knowledge, this agent has never made a cold call. He was 30 years old when he came into the business and in his second year made over $100,000. He is still going strong and still doing it the easy way!

What's next?

So you've got a book full of appointments with people you know and like, and who like you. That's important. Remember this: People do business with people they like. The next logical question is a panic-stricken "Now what?"

For starters, don't rush right into your sales talk. Take a few minutes and tell your friend how you decided to come into the insurance business. Tell him about all the "job" interviews that just didn't seem like the right place to spend your life. Tell him about your concerns about climbing the corporate ladder with someone else conducting periodic subjective reviews of your performance. Talk about the thought process that led you to decide to go into business for yourself, and how, with limited capital commitment and unlimited income potential, the insurance business always surfaced as the best opportunity. Talk about your interviews with your new company and how impressed you were. Communicate your enthusiasm and commitment!

When you have done all of that and you and your friend are relaxed, ask him if he would mind listening to the kind of work you do. (He won't mind.) Give your sales talk, and when it is finished ask if it makes sense. (It will.) Tell your friend you would like to work for him. You are essentially applying for the job as his or her insurance agent. You are on your way! Believe me, this works. It works every time as far as getting appointments goes. You will also make a lot of sales. In the next chapter we'll discuss branching out to your friends' friends.

Don't forget what this chapter is all about:

- You must have activity.
- Plan on selling no less than 100 lives each year.
- The more you sell, the better you will be at selling.
- Focus on the job at hand: Focus on prospecting, focus on selling.
- Do it the easy way!
- People do business with people they like.
- Communicate your commitment and enthusiasm.
- Apply for the job as your friends' insurance agent.

Chapter 9

Referrals

Do you remember the trick kids used to play on each other about getting a penny from someone and just doubling the money every day?

Did you read about the judge who fined a city in New York State $500, and doubled the fine every day until it complied with his ruling? Well, that city, Yonkers, had to get an injunction to stop the fine or it would have been bankrupt in less than a month.

Referrals work the same way. Think about this. You land in a faraway city where you only know one person. You go to see him and get two referrals. Then you go to those two people and get two more from each. How many prospects would you have if you repeated this exercise just eight times? Put your calculator away! The number is 511! Is that incredible? If you start getting referrals right away, you will never make a cold call, never talk to anyone with whom you have nothing in common. Let me tell you, folks, this is a lot nicer business when you do it that way. You could actually have too many people to call on.

"People Don't Like Giving Referrals"

I guess you have heard this claim before. Maybe you have even said it. I'd like to know who made up this "rule." Was it a marginal or failing salesman or a policy peddler? Did he bring any added value to the relationship? Did the client get anything he couldn't have gotten from Baby Food Life Insurance? Haven't you seen the ads for Gerber Life? "No salesman will call! Send in the application form." No one refused. Gerber Life doesn't get referrals and doesn't need them. You do!

In order to be able to expect referrals, you have to give a service beyond just selling a policy. I'm not saying you have to have done a major estate plan or business analysis. You may have done nothing more than explain the economic, common-sense necessity of a good disability-income policy. That is a value added. Maybe you have brought the fellow around to thinking about the value of forced savings or the impact of even modest inflation on his family's standard of living. That is value added. You have done something over and above. He has reason to suggest that other people talk to you. You make sense!

Isn't that the way all referrals work? When you get superior service, treatment or advice from a mechanic, attorney or doctor, aren't you quick to tell all your friends about it? Of course you are, because you want to let all your friends in on a good thing. Why should the situation be any different with financial advice?

The answer is that it shouldn't be any different. If you do something good for people and they recognize it and appreciate it, they will tell other people about you. Now I'm sure that just because you do something good, people are not going to run out into the highways and byways screaming out your name. You will have to prompt them a little. This is where a lot of agents make mistakes. They don't know how to ask for referrals. Let's talk about that.

"Well, thank you very much, Harry; put your policy in a safe place, and, if you have any questions, please feel free to call. By the way, do you know anyone else I could call on?" Wrong! Wrong! Wrong! Harry's mind will turn to mush. He not only won't know anybody you can call on, he won't know anybody at all!

The referral process begins with the first interview and never stops. In the approach talk I learned as a new agent, I told the prospect I was paid in two ways. First, if my analysis indicated he had a need for an insurance product, he would buy it from me; second, if he thought the work I did was of value, he would refer me to others.

Maybe you don't like those words. OK, change them. Use any words you like, but get your message across: You work on a referral basis.

Here are some other ways to prepare your soon-to-be client for the referral process.

"You know, Jim, in my business what sets people apart from the crowd is competence and service. I want to spend all my time serving the people who do business with me, and keeping current with the latest developments that might impact on their situations. If I have to spend a lot of time finding people to talk to, the service to valued clients like yourself will have to suffer. That is why from time to time I'm going to ask you for introductions to other people who could use my help."

"Jack, in my business, like so many others, inventory is crucial. Unlike so many other businesses, I can't just call a supplier and buy more inventory. You see, my inventory is people. If I am to remain successful, and be here to service your needs for a long time, I'll need a constant supply of new people to call on. I have to rely on people who already know me and the kind of work that I do to keep me supplied with a new inventory of people."

"Lou, I think you'll agree that what we have done here is important." Of course he will. "From time to time I'd like to help you identify other people among your business and social acquaintances who would benefit from this kind of work."

That is a reasonable sampling of the words. You can put it to your own music and run with it. Change the words around. Use some, and discard others. Mix and match to your heart's content. Remember, referrals make the business a lot easier. When you work on a referral basis, you spend less time getting appointments and more time selling and servicing. Referrals are as important to your clients as they are to you. The less time you have to spend prospecting, the more time you have for your clients.

Identifying the Prospects

OK, everyone agrees to refer you. Now who do you want to see? What is your client profile? What market are you in? Are you in a particular market at all, or are you a generalist?

Simply put, you ought to know what kind of people you want to talk to before you ask for referrals from your clients. If you are in the young-singles or young-marrieds market, then you have to help your clients identify people they know in those categories.

If you are in one market and want to move to another, be sure you know exactly what you want in the other category. For example, some agents in the personal or family market decide they want to be in the business market. They ask for referrals to businesses, and a client gives them the name of a vice president he knows at some firm with 8,000 employees. By the way, the referral is one of 200 vice presidents. The agent didn't get what he wanted. He didn't get the right referral because he didn't properly identify the kind of business he had in mind.

If you want a business with no more than 10 or 20 employees, *say so.*

If you want a business with no more than two or three owners, *say so.*

If you want to talk to people who have just started a business, *say so.*

If you want to talk to successful businesspeople who are making money and may have a tax problem and need some tax relief, *say so.*

If you want to talk to people just starting their first jobs, or young marrieds with kids, or without kids, or if you want to talk to one-income or two-income families, *say so.*

You see, it is entirely up to you to define your preferred market. When you make up your mind where you are most comfortable working, just concentrate on being referred to those kinds of people. No one is comfortable in all situations, and we all function best where we are most comfortable.

How Do You Like Your Eggs?

Not everyone likes their eggs the same way and not everyone likes the same mechanics when it comes to referrals. Let me give you a few ideas that have worked for others. Hopefully, you'll be able to use one.

An agent I once knew used to bring a form to his clients that looked like this:

My Ten-Best List

The ten most promising young businesspeople I know are:

Name	Age	Business	Phone	Income
1.				
2.				
3.				
4.				
5.				
6.				
7.				
8.				
9.				
10.				

Signed by: _____

This worked for him time and time again. That was all he wanted. He then told his client that he was going to call on these people, and asked if the client would mind his telling the folks on the list how highly the client thought of them. This young man made the $5 Million Forum of the Million Dollar Round Table when he was only 24 years old. That was 1971!

How about this? I was once referred to a man who owned a pet shop. One Saturday morning I went out to see him and sold my first Keogh plan (which included a good-sized life-insurance policy) and a DI policy. I explained the importance of referrals as clearly as possible amid the barking, meowing and chirping that was going on. He said, "Sure, Joe, I'll give you some referrals, get out your pad." He proceeded to give me the names of about 25 pet-shop owners in the New York City area.

Needless to say, I was pretty excited. I went home and told my wife what had happened, and she asked me what I was going to do with all those names. She wanted to know if I had any specific plan for dealing with all those people. I didn't have a clue. It was my first year in the business, and I guess I was a little overcome by the number of referrals. I went back to the pet shop and asked my new client if he would call these people for me. No way! I asked him if he would sign a letter of introduction if I wrote it up. He said yes.

Now I needed something quick, simple, to the point and, hopefully, effective. Sending out letters didn't appeal to me. It never has. Then I got an idea that I've used from time to time since then. Others have also used it with success.

I took a whole bunch of business cards and on the back typed the following message, inserting the first name of each referral in the salutation:

Hi _____

Take 20 minutes to talk to Joe
Casale. He tells a hell of a story.

Best regards, _____

I brought these cards back to my client, and he signed them all. I then broke the referrals down geographically so I could call on as many people in one day as possible. I didn't want to be going from one end of New York City to the other and back again. Then I simply went out and called on those people. When I walked into their shops and they asked if they could help me, I simply told them I had a message from a friend of theirs, and handed them the card. When they turned the card over, they saw who I worked for and what I did. I sold a few of those people and I probably screwed up a lot more of the interviews because of inexperience, but I've always liked the business-card note as an introduction to a referral.

The Rolls Royce Referral

While it is surely true that any method of referral is better than no referral at all, there is, I think, one best way to get referrals. I learned this from the fellow who was the leading agent in the first agency I worked in. His line went something like this: "Jim, as I've mentioned, I need referrals to stay in business. Unlike many other agents, I'm not going to ask you to fill up a book with the names of everybody you know. I'd like to discuss with you some of your top business associates. They could be customers of yours or competitors. They just might be good friends who have businesses of their own. When we have talked about them for a while, I'll tell you which ones I think I can help the most. Then I'd like you to call them and tell them about me and ask when they can see me. I have my appointment book right here. If you'd prefer, once they have agreed to see me I'll get on the phone and make the appointment."

He really did that. I saw him do it time and time again. It was the old "assumed consent" philosophy at

work. Boy, did it work. This fellow had been successful in business before coming into the insurance business. When he filled out his prospect list, he had 500
names. (I had 12, remember?) I once asked him if he
ever got through the list. He never got past the first 50!
He didn't have to. He had Rolls Royce referrals. By the
way, for the last 20 years or so he has driven a Rolls
Royce, too!

Remember these points:

- Do it any way that works for you, but get on a
  referral basis.
- Don't put it off.
- Don't be afraid to ask.
- Earn your referral by the quality of your work.

Chapter 10

Different Strokes

The chapter on referrals makes it pretty clear how I feel about referrals. I also know that some people are never going to ask for them. Others will ask very infrequently. Still others will hint around the subject, hoping the client will somehow volunteer a thousand names.

The people who don't get referrals and are still reasonably successful are doing something with which they are comfortable. I know a lot of agents like that. Let's discuss some of the methods they use.

Cold Telephone Calls

This one kills me. I hate to make calls to people I don't know. Yet, some agents use this method almost to the exclusion of every other. One of the most successful agents in my agency is still making cold calls on a daily basis. He has been in the business 12 years, and in recent years has seldom done less than $100,000 in first-year commissions.

Most of the folks using this method buy either lists or cards from Dun and Bradstreet. These typically show the name and address of the business, the nature of the business, number of employees, CEO and the telephone number. You can order these cards within specific demographic parameters. For example, when our agency was doing a lot of business in the small-group market, we ordered the cards for every business with fewer than ten employees in Manhattan, Queens, and the Bronx that had been in business less than two years. Subsequently we changed the description and ordered again. You can vary by retail and wholesale, manufacturing or sales, and just about any parameters you can think of.

The bottom line is, however: You still don't know them or they you.

Direct Mail

A lot of agents do direct mail. They seem to favor the kind with reply cards. It sounds pretty good. You send out a bunch of letters describing what you have to offer, and, if the prospects are interested, they return the reply card and you call them for an appointment. Can it work? Sure! The problem is that most agents either can't afford to, or don't want to, send out the tremendous quantities of mail that it requires to be successful with this system.

Another problem with many company-sponsored direct-mail programs is that they invariably offer some "free gift" to those who reply. Naturally, you get plenty of people who are just looking for a gift. Why not?

The fellow I know who was most successful with direct mail sent out at least 5,000 letters each month. He called all the repliers, and he continued to mail to the nonrepliers because he felt that eventually he would sell them all. He's very successful. It works for him. If you can afford it, try it.

If you send everything out first class, you are going to spend about $15,000 a year on postage. And you're spending it on people you don't know.

Cold Calling in Person

A young man in my agency uses this method almost exclusively. He has been with us only three years and has been reasonably successful. He doesn't look like Robert Redford and he is no smarter than the rest of us, but he is a likable guy, low-key but persistent, and he hates making phone calls.

Believe it or not, if tomorrow Congress passed a law banning the giving or receiving of referrals, this is the method of prospecting I'd use. I have more confidence in myself in person than I do in my voice on the phone. It isn't that I have any hang-ups about my voice. It is simply that the human condition makes it more difficult to turn a person away cold when he or she is standing in front of you. Hanging up the phone, on the other hand, is a cinch. In person, you have a chance to develop an instant chemistry with your prospect. Haven't you ever met someone for the first time whom you liked immediately? That can happen with cold calling as well.

All the Rest

Invariably, when I talk to a group about prospecting, someone will say, "Hey, Joe, you didn't mention ——!" (Fill in the blank.) My gut feeling is that everything else falls into one or more of these categories. For example, consider "social prospecting": You involve yourself in one or more community activities, such as Little League, Kiwanis, a church group. You get to know a lot of people, they get to know you and what you do, and pretty soon you are talking business. This is pretty close to a self-referral. Either you have referred yourself to the prospects or they have referred themselves to you. I have an extraordinary example of this kind of thing. My golf club.

I took up golf when I was 47 years old. One day I hated it; it was a game for sissies. The next day I was hooked. Almost immediately I joined a golf club. I knew only a handful of people besides the two fellows who sponsored me. One day a fellow I didn't know came up and asked me if I was Joe Casale. I said yes. He said, "I've been involved in some business with Bill Adams, and he asked me to look for you at the club because you were a new member." He told me his name, and said, "I understand you are in the insurance business and know something about pensions." One thing led to another; and over the course of the next year, although I never did put in a pension plan for him, I sold his company about $7 million of whole life and an executive salary continuation plan.

The following March I stopped by the club on a cold, rainy Saturday morning just to see who was around. One of the members whom I knew very casually came up to where I was drinking a cup of coffee and asked how I was doing. I said fine, and he asked me what business I was in. I told him. He said that maybe I could help him. I did put a pension plan in his company, and disability, and just last year a substantial stock-redemption plan. Oh God, I wish I had taken up golf 20 years ago! In a little over two years I sold the equivalent of $10 million of whole life to people I had never laid eyes on until I joined that club. And remember, I never asked anybody to talk business. They all asked me.

I hope this short treatise on prospecting methods other than referrals helps. I often tell my young single agents about my experience at my golf club. I know they are in the habit of spending a lot of money on their social lives and I think it would be better spent at a golf club, where they could socialize and meet the kinds of people who make great clients.

Chapter 11

Between the Cracks

It is inevitable that when you undertake something like this book there are going to be some things you wish you had said or some topics you wish you had covered. As I read the manuscript, I realized there were a few more things I'd like to say to new agents as well as to experienced ones. So here are a few topics selected at random that may have fallen between the cracks.

Time Control

One of the hardest things about our business is that you are not working the eight-to-four shift at Ford's

Dearborn plant. There is no clock to punch you in and no whistle to tell you when to punch out. You and only you decide when you are going to work and when you are going to loaf, play, hide, rest.

Unless you are a professional athlete, work and play seldom come at the same time. I say "seldom" with the golf course in mind. It goes without saying that getting an early start on the day is a must for any agent who hopes to be successful. There is a lot to do. Consider.

You Have To Study

If you aren't current on the things affecting your business, your clients and prospects will soon find out, and, friends or not, they will think less of you. Believe me, I have taken over as insurance agent for some firms whose previous agent was "a good guy and a friend" but "just didn't know his stuff."

You Have To Prepare and Review Your Presentations for the Day

Complete preparedness and clarity of presentation are givens with all highly successful professionals, not just insurance salesmen.

You Have To Call for Appointments

Whether it is a new referral or a service call on an existing client, the calls have to be made.

You Have To Handle Your Correspondence

Even if you have an excellent secretary, you have to deal with what is important to you and your clients. The absence of your personal involvement does not go unnoticed for very long.

You Have To Sell

That's what it's all about, Alfie!

So is it any wonder, then, that an early start is an essential first step to time control? There are two major distractions that have to be dealt with: interruptions and the telephone.

Interruptions

You have two choices: Keep your door closed and put a Do Not Disturb sign on it. Or . . . leave it open and, if people barge in, politely tell them you are busy and will have to see them later. The latter choice gives you the option of deciding whether you want to be interrupted or not. The former leaves the decision as to the importance of the visit up to the person at the door. Both methods work. Take your pick.

The Telephone

You can't do business without a phone these days, but

it can drive you crazy. Once again, I'll give you two choices:

A. If you have someone to answer your phone, give him or her a select list of calls you will take that morning. (You should have some idea of what issues might require your immediate attention.) Ask your assistant to tell all other callers that you will be out of the office until 11 o'clock, and to add, "May he call you then?" Then at 11 o'clock, *return all calls.*

If you do not have a secretary or assistant to answer your phone, try to do what I've described above through your receptionist or telephone operator. If that is impossible, here is plan B.

B. Answer the phone and find out who it is. If you decide that you can't take the time to talk to that person at that time, simply say, "Hey, it is great to hear from you. I'm in the middle of something right now. Could I call you back at 11, or is it something urgent?" If it is urgent, talk. If not, call back at 11.

I recognize that the phone rings in the afternoon, too. The same procedures apply. Just decide what time you want to return phone calls.

Organization

I'm only talking about personal organization here as it applies to your business. Everybody has a different method and a different philosophy; use whatever works best for you.

Organizing Your Activity

I say keep it simple. Buy one of those "At a Glance" date books. They come by the day, week or month. Choose whichever one suits you best. Then buy one of those pads that say "Things To Do Today." They look like this:

Things To Do Today

In your appointment or date book keep your notations on who, where, when and why for each appointment. On your "Today" sheet put down in order of importance those things that have to be accomplished that day.

To the extent that you complete what you want for the day you are successful. If there were some things that simply could not be completed that day, carry them over to the next day, again in their order of relative importance.

There are all kinds of "executive organizers" on the market today and they are all wonderful *if* you use them. I have one I got as a "free" gift for subscribing to a business magazine. It really is a nice item, but I wouldn't want to carry it around all day. It is too bulky to put in my pocket and I don't want to carry a briefcase everywhere I go. I decided to leave it on my desk and use it there. Monthly plans, daily reminders, telephone numbers and so on are all in there. When I figure out a way to make it thin enough to carry around, it will be perfect. It really is not ideal for the desk, either, because it is a little too small and you have to write in microscopic letters. I'll probably trash it.

Telephone Numbers

I used to carry one of those very small telephone books in my wallet, but I found my wallet getting bulkier and bulkier. I took it out and wrote down the most important unmemorized numbers on a 4" × 6" sheet of plain white paper. I folded it and stuck that in my wallet.

Expenses

If you have an American Express card, you can just keep your expense notations in your big appointment book and American Express will send you a quarterly report of expenses as well as your monthly statement with copies of all your receipts. If you want to really nail down your expense record keeping, clip or staple a copy of your receipt into your book on the page where the appropriate date appears. If you don't have a credit card that gives you detailed statements, this is the best way to keep your expense records. Remember, you need to know who, what, where, why, when, and the percentage of expense attributable to business. Most of that information can be filled in on the back of a credit-card charge slip.

Computers

Except for certain pension documents, buy-sell agreements, wills and trusts that I happen to have copies of, all of my client files are on the same lap-top computer that I have written this book on. I hate files, and I hate paper. As soon as I discover a suitable scanner that can read documents to my hard disk, I won't even have the above-mentioned papers.

Policy Illustrations

In those cases where I have shown an insured a home-office computer-generated illustration of the policy he or she is buying, I write the insured's name, the policy number and the date of the policy on the illustration and put it in a looseleaf binder in alphabetical order. Once again, when I get a scanner, that looseleaf book will be history.

Selling Price and Product

In this age of consumerism everybody is talking about life insurance as an investment. People are talking about rates of return and so on. It is not all bad. People are entitled to reasonable value for their money. But with so much of their sales pitches based on *nonguaranteed* dividends and interest rates, I wish companies and agents put more emphasis on their value and not the product.

Think about this . . .

THE HIGHEST-PRODUCING AGENTS HARDLY EVER COME FROM THE COMPANIES WITH THE "BEST" PRODUCTS.

Do you know why that is? BECAUSE THE REALLY GREAT AGENTS SELL THEMSELVES, NOT THE PRICE OR THE PRODUCT.

Divorced Parents

Unfortunately, these days divorce is prevalent in our society. What do you do for these folks? Well, there is usually a court-ordered division of responsibilities. So, very simply, work with each parent, first in accordance with his or her obligations, and then go on to discuss his or her desires. In chapter 5, you'll find a discussion of financial planning for singles and for married folks with and without children. The principles you find there apply just the same here. Each parent is part of a family and, if they don't remarry, single at the same time.

Retirees and Those About to Retire

Both of these groups need very careful counseling. They are concerned about having enough money to retire and about having enough once they retire to last their lifetimes. These are delicate subjects and need great sensitivity on our part. If you don't know enough about money to handle this, get help from someone who does.

The person about to retire usually has a couple of options. One is to take less pension so that his or her spouse will receive something at the retiree's death for the remainder of the spouse's life. The other is to take the maximum pension and take a chance that the spouse will either not outlive the retiree or can provide in some other fashion. This is where insurance comes into play.

If a man could take a maximum pension of $2,000 per month instead of a joint and survivor pension of $1,500 per month, he might be able to use some or all of the difference for a limited number of years to buy enough insurance to provide his wife with what she would have received as a survivor benefit.

Let's say that if he elected joint and survivor he and his wife would have gotten $1,500 per month while both were still alive, but his wife would have gotten only $1,000 per month (two-thirds) after his death. He is giving up $500 per month to assure his wife a life income.

Assuming six percent return, a man could buy $200,000 of life insurance with part of the difference. He would then have the higher income while he was alive, and his wife would be no worse off at his death than if he had elected the joint and survivor pension. Six percent of $200,000 is $12,000—the same $1,000 per month the survivor benefit was going to pay.

For people already retired, the benefit option has 'been made. Find out what it is and, if it was maximum pension, explore the couple's feelings about what the wife will do if she survives. If there is concern, proceed as described above. If the couple took the survivor option, talk to them about how they are doing and see if you can find some way to make them more secure.

Epilogue

That is about it. I started out to write a short no-nonsense booklet on insurance sales made simple and wound up with over 100 pages. I am told it is still short as books go. I hope so.

If it helps someone have a clearer understanding of what we do, then I'll count the book a success.

If it helps an agent persevere through a barrage of objections without substance, that will be great.

And if it helps agents make a few more sales, well, that's why I wrote the book.

Appendix

Common-Sense Quadrant

For: _____ Age: _____

Spouse's name: _____ Age: _____

Children's ages: __ __ __ __ __

Occupation: _____ Spouse's occupation: _____

Are you self-employed? _____
  (If yes, use business section
  for details.)

Monthly expenses: _____ Monthly savings: _____

Annual family income: _____

Source: _____

ALL PLANNING BEGINS WITH WHAT YOU HAVE AND IS CAR-
RIED OUT BASED ON WHAT YOU WANT.

Investments	Other
Stocks Bonds Mutual funds Real estate Commodities Metals Pension IRA Personal property $_____ Your feelings?	Insurance from employer Inheritances, trusts $_____ Your feelings?
Cash	**Insurance**

Money market
CDs
T bills
Etc.
 	
$_____
 	
Your feelings?
	Life insurance
	  Personal $_____
	  Business $_____
	Your feelings?
	
	Disability income (permanent)
	$_____/month
	Your feelings?

© Joe Casale

111

Estate Questions

1. Do you have a will? _____ What kind? _____
2. Do you have a trust? _____ What kind? _____
   (Pick up wills and trusts whenever possible.)
3. When was your will drawn? _____ Your trust? _____
4. What are your feelings about the disposition of your estate?

_____

_____

5. Are you aware of the impact of estate taxes on your estate? _____
   (Show tax table.)
6. What are your feelings about inflation?

_____

7. What do you consider a reasonable net rate of return? _____

Business Questions

1. Do you own a business? _____ Year started? _____
   Sole Proprietorship   Partnership   S Corporation
   Registered Corporation   (Circle one.)
   Fiscal year ____ % Ownership ____ No. of partners ____
   (Get details.)
   Tax ID No. _____ State of incorporation _____
2. Do you value your business annually? ____
   Worth last valuation? _____
3. Do you have a business agreement? ____ When was it done? _____
4. No. of employees ____ What fringe benefits do you provide?
   Group medical insurance Yes____ No____
   Group DI Insurance Yes____ No____
   Pension/Profit sharing Yes____ No____ (Get data and/or plan
                                            info on each benefit.)
5. Regarding benefits you do not provide, why not?_____

_____

6. Are you using your business to help you accumulate wealth?

_____

Asset	Value	Insured Amount	Premium
Home	⎯⎯	⎯⎯	⎯⎯
Cars	⎯⎯	⎯⎯	⎯⎯
Jewelry, furs, etc.	⎯⎯	⎯⎯	⎯⎯
Level income to age 65	⎯⎯	⎯⎯	⎯⎯

Based on the conversation we have just had, let's talk about some things you want to accomplish and the assets that might be needed to accomplish them.

What You Want	What It Costs

Index